CW01649973

I dedicate this book to the abstemiouses.

To all people who do not drink wine

due to the not immediate pleasantness of its taste.

And I do this while hoping that day after day

wine may find always new, enthusiastic

and passionate consumers thanks to this work

and becoming more pleasant

No abstemiouses with wines with high Index of

Pleasantness.

No abstemiouses with the Wine-Fruit.

Let's enter the glass

INTRODUCTION

No book, however valid, means what it illustrates as the direct experience of each of us.
Nothing more than experimenting is fundamental for complete knowing.

So in this book I will tell the results of my experience of professional taster – begun 11 years ago – to provide all wine lovers with the method and the basic technical notions to become professionals in wine tasting.

Then it will be up to each of you to effectively become professional tasters since, in order to be able to fully taste a wine - besides method and basic technical notions - it is necessary to practice: in other words to taste.

Abstemious until 24 years old (I did not find pleasant the taste of wine for its strong acidity and bitterness which rarely gave room to the very pleasant sugary softness of grape), I said to myself that I wanted, I had to become a wine "expert". And therefore I did have to appreciate that taste even forcing myself. I decided that I had to learn how to subdue and appreciate that taste. Passage that naturally results unnatural to most people: from here the many abstemiouses and the few fans of wine amongst the young. So I became fond of wine and I madly begun loving it. I studied wine in depth for more than 5 years on university texts on winegrowing, oenology, and taste physiology.

I loved wine so much as to drink it with joy and total passion even without appreciating its taste with my senses. An intellectual relationship more than a sensorial one.

The first time I found myself in front of a glass of wine in order to evaluate its quality, I only had a great theoretical knowledge of wine, I had been drinking many wines as a lover and no one as a critic. I did not precisely know what "quality of wine" consisted on, I did not have references or a method to measure it. And this despite the lots of read books: a great deal of more or less abstract information, but no one precise definition of the quality of wine, no method to concretely evaluate it. I did not know what to do in front of that glass. I did not have any means to do what I desperately wanted to. A sensation of impotence, of total block. I was simply annihilated, deeply humiliated.

I committed myself to this task: succeeding in knowing wine so well as to understand what its quality consisted on and to create an effective method by which all of us could measure it.

I push my way more deeply into the tale, opening to sensations.

When I breathed in my first glass of wine, the olfactory wave coming up was dark. Solid black. There was a lot inside it but I just could not understand and evaluate what that wave was carrying. I could only feel if the overall smell was pleasant or not. The same olfactory wave inhaled by me today is incredibly full of significance and of sensible (and detectable) facets. Pure clearness. Not only the overall pleasantness, but also nature and technical measure of it. With great clearness of details and sensorial shades.

This for the taste, for the mass of gustative and tactile sensations which is the passage of a sip into the mouse. Yesterday the taste was a compact, indistinct, an unvaried whole. Narrow tube, more or less good. Today the taste distinctively hands me the measure and the harmony of diverse constitutive elements of wine working to generate wide, distinct and varied flavours on the buttons of the tongue. Open cone, not only the overall pleasantness, but also the nature and the technical measure of it. With great clearness of details and sensorial shades.

But as regards to that first time, my judgement on a same wine has not changed at all: a wine that then did not result pleasant to my senses, is felt today even less pleasant The same occurs for the pleasant wines today appreciated even more in depth. But now I reckon with great evidence the technical reason why does a given wine result more or less pleasant. Today I can give a true measure of its objective pleasantness: in other words I know how to analytically argue the qualitative judgement of a given wine.

Let's always have in mind what follows: if wine does not produce pleasantness at tasting, the fault does not belong to a taster incapable of properly tasting, the fault belongs to the wine surely deficient in quality. Any wine proves itself to the senses of the taster and/or the drinker thanks to its chemical-physical composition. If a wine is rich in components in fair qualitative equilibrium, if it is devoid of defective constituents and decrepit parts, if in practice it is chemically and physically (analytically) qualitative, its taste can only be pleasant. The opposite can never be true.

But then abstemiouses are right. And if they do not appreciate wine it is not responsibility of their ignorance; wine often does not have a pleasant taste because it lacks of quality. Therefore anyone who loves wine must always respect the abstemiouses for their demand of pleasant wines, for their demand of good wines under the technical and qualitative point of view.

The quality of a wine is definitely the pleasantness of its taste.

The Index of Quality coincides with the Index of Pleasantness because only grapes with perfect chemical-physical composition, transformed into wine in a technically perfect manner, may generate wines with pleasant taste. Not vice versa.

Any individual is therefore universally able of perceiving analytical Index of Quality of wine, being any individual naturally capable of perceiving the Index of Pleasantness of wine.

Everyone perceives the same taste in the same way; as far as functionality of the sense organ is concerned, every one of us is a perfect taster. Thanks to his technical knowledge and experience, the professional taster is besides able to argue in detail his sensorial evaluation; occasional drinkers and/or abstemious who know a little of wine technique and do not have tasting experience cannot do the same. So the abstemious exactly feels what taster and all other people perceive, but he is not able to explain what and how much he likes of a certain wine, or even why. The professional taster is a sensorial analyst. The one who evaluates and argue in depth the perceived through a careful technical examination of the registered sensations.

So thinking "I understand nothing about wine, I don't know how to taste" is a huge mistake. It would be as saying that one cannot realise if any gastronomic dish is pleasant, well prepared and obtained from first quality raw material. If in a restaurant we are given a course of burnt pasta or meat, if it is insipid or rancid, we discuss it with the restaurateur, going deeply into the matter of perceived defects. No one of us would even think of attending a course for pasta tasting, or visiting a meat producer to learn how to understand (!) meat culture.

So it really is a blunder to drink and appreciate wines through/with brain. It is wrong because all the consumers in the world – fairly and naturally – appreciate wine through/with senses: they drink wine if wine is good, they do not drink it if it is not good. They do not drink wine if its taste is unpleasant, in other words if its analytical quality is poor.

Therefore it is wrong to intellectively enjoy wine as I used to do at the beginning of my experience, and as some "experts" still do. For these people wine is nourishment whatever taste it might have. For these people the quality of wine is and must remain an obscure question, prerogative of few chosens. To those "experts" important elements are complexity, finesse, elegance, typicalness, nobility (and so on, always more abstrusely, always more distant from the truth and the universal comprehensibility). In fact experience proves that during tasting wines with high Index of Pleasantness, wines recalling constitutive fruit, are unanimously recognised as the best wines, wines of best quality. Everyone likes them; with no exception and for these wines recalling the fruit - for Wine-Fruit – the abstemiouses do not exist. (For these wines also wine-alcoholics will not exist any more because it does not come to abuse a pleasant drink to harm oneself).

So the tasting is not an art or a talent. It is a technical discipline the practice of which allows measuring, evaluating, describing and analytically arguing what any individual's senses perfectly and naturally register at the contact with a certain wine.

The first thought arrived to my mind while attentively feeling the taste of a wine was appropriate: how is it possible that a drink obtained from grape – universally pleasant – does not taste as the fruit it is made of? How is it possible that a wine would not reveal during tasting the pleasantness – consistent, balanced and integral – of the ripe grape just picked from the plant and immediately tasted?

For what said to this point, this is possible because, yesterday more than today, it was rare to meet a wine so technically perfect as to result sensorially pleasant. And this for two reasons: 1) because it is objectively difficult and very expensive to produce excellent grapes and transform it into excellent wines (now possible a thing thanks to the very recent, incredible technical progress made by viticulture and oenology). 2) Because producers, not reproved by the above mentioned "experts" - uncritical critics, complicated and complicating people – diverted their minds from the taste of the wine and made their best efforts so that the abstractly appreciable qualities of their wines were highlighted far more than their universally perceivable limits.

This was. This is and this will be, all the more, less.

On my behalf, I would like very much to apologise with all the peoples who – being in sensorial right – have been humiliated by us "experts" with the accusation or the thought that they understood nothing on wine for the simple reason that they did not recognise quality to the wines whose taste did not result pleasant.

And even more I would like to testify with this book of mine the renewed, total commitment of the world of wine for a production always more universally pleasant, for a wine more and more truly and comprehensibly illustrated and evaluated.

The humility necessary to recognise and overcome its past limits is proper of the nature and the secular tradition of wine.

This is why I am writing this book: to render everyone able of knowing and understanding the relation wine-senses. To render each and every one able to understand why and how much he likes a certain wine. To render each and every one able to feel and describe the quality of a wine, appreciating and entirely loving it. Doing this for the sake of wine. Because it is certain: qualitative improvement of any product passes through the improvement of consumer's faculties of estimation. Consumer's specialisation renders substantially inevitable to producer the analytical and technical optimisation of the product. If no one knows in what quality of wine consists on and how to measure it, all the wines are good of course, or only the ones indicated by the "experts" will be so. On the other hand, if we shall all be able of evaluating substantial quality of wine, wines will all have to be qualitative, the whole of them will have to result undistinctively pleasant to anyone who would taste them.

Then, no one would answer to the question "do you like this wine?" as it happens today: "I am not that keen on wines, I am not an expert".
No one would then answer this way because with wines with high Index of Pleasantness we naturally are all true experts.

CHAPTER I

SENSORIAL ANALYSIS AND WINE

ANALYSING SENSATIONS TO EVALUATE AND DESCRIBE THEM

To analyse sensations means to think of them. Sensations must be thought and can be narrated; you cannot describe sensations that had not been thought.

When you describe sensations, you describe what you feel.
Everything is very fast, sort of "united".
You make what you have to in order to feel; you think and analyse what you have felt through asking yourself questions, then you can narrate it.

In order to feel and to think what you feel you have to be very attentive, with sensors and thought well stretched out. In this way you exercise your humanity, which is capacity of thinking the perceived and feeling the thought.
Thus very high consistency, equilibrium and integrity may generate.

Everything that moves our senses reaches through them a particular point where everything converges and that particular point receives, registers, inspires, focuses, introjects, melts, amalgamates, units, understands – perceives – everything. From that point everything then departs as perceived, evaluated, dismantled, articulated, weighed, thought, known.
This point is between eyes and mind. It is named man and it is where our nature identifies herself.
There you see through your eyes, hear and smell with ears and nose; there you think the sense of touch, and taste also – on the highest vault of the palate; there you can perceive.

For a good thinking and feeling, you must breath. The breath nourishes the attention. Attention raises sensorial power, feeds reception and elaboration, and energises senses and mind in their very deep and very fast process of connective conduction.

To narrate and describe sensations, the sensible thought itself must write. Let's give sensations a pen. One must find the best, the most musical, the most suasive way of describing and narrating what one has felt. It is not difficult; in fact it is very beautiful and amusing. You cannot be but true. Everyone naturally can do it well. Through time and the repeated one self's application, each one will succeed in adhering better to the nature of what he felt. In other words to the nature of what thanks to its existence was contacted. The language is just a descriptive tool. Let's use it this way. Let's shape it into and on the perceived with an exemplifying ductility with no equals; no restraints on the perceived and no restraints on the described. Nature is maximum possible freedom. If a smell is good let's say it, if it has merits let's narrate them, if it has defects let's describe them. Let's talk about flavour, its composition and resolution pointed out by taste. Let's try to penetrate the nature of what was felt in order to render it well detailed in the narration as a faithful explicative memory of the contact.
To describe sensation with the writing is only possible through attention, which allows the perfect reception and extension of the sensible thought.

Subjects of this vital action must be the breath and the attention.
Breath and attention, for man capacity of.

THE COLOUR OF WINE

Under a beam of illuminating light let's gaze a few times and from different points of view the colour of wine. Let's move wine inside the glass to see it; let's put wine under different light zones. With the whole of these attentions, let's see this and a lot more about the colour of wine.
Intensity of colour: how strong is the colour; let's search it very well, count pigments, whose density gives the strength of the hue. Let's focus eye and mind on the point where we are looking. Let's evaluate the intensity of transparency, which is the opposite of the colour.
Shades of hue: which timber does the colour have, which point, state, tone does the illuminating molecule have? Which border and remote colours have been touched by the hue? Is this lively or is it loading with dark and not integral yellowness?
Density of hue: let's see how the richness of wine components facilitate or brake its movement in the glass. Let's evaluate the duration and the weigh of the extractive wakes on the crystal surface. Let's evaluate the visual oiliness of wine.

THE PARFUME OF WINE

It is necessary to breathe in deeply with eyes shut and not to stop at first contact, but to strongly prolong inhalation. Let's bring the air flux - rendered by alcohol incomparably penetrating, supporting and heady - exactly to the eye centre. And let's enjoy it, focusing on the detail we want to study, on both quality and quantity of the perfume and let us quickly compare a few times the perfumes of all the examined wines. Let's enter the glass with our nose so that agent-wine and receptor-nose may nearly touch. Let's offer the nostrils transversally to wine disk and not straight so that a greater portion of sensible surface will evaluate inspired stream. Rotate a few times wine inside glass, so that the aromatic substances may well and abundantly volatilize. Repeat the inspiration all the times necessary to seize everything possible, in order to exhaust the wine with the nose. Let's smell the perfume of wine with eyes shut and remember it.

With these attentions, perceive this and even more of the perfume of wine.

Intensity of the perfume: any subsequent time, we shall smell the same perfume with less strength and clearness, but progressively smelling and re-smelling it we'll better understand its volume and expressive power: the more or less magnificent alcoholic power which renders its mass that incisive.

Density of the perfume: the mantle, the stream thickness, and its olfactory weight, its smelling touch. Is the stream airy or gummy, dry or mellow, diluted or plump?

Shape of the perfume: when the end of the nose is touched, does inhaled perfume stream acutely dull or does it roundly wrap? Is it staying spherical thanks to the equilibrium of the thrusts and the opposite dimensions of sweetness, acidity and bitterness? Is it concave or convex? Is it acute due to excess of peaks, or flat for lack of savouriness and strength?

The contents of the perfume: what am I smelling?

Basic and shaded tendency of the perfume: what is this perfume like? Acid, bitter, salty, sweet. Balanced. Fruity. Turgid. Fresh, hot, soft, mellow, "passito", rancid, sugary, sulphureous, acetous, milky, vanished, ligneous, faded.

Structure and shades of the perfume: the perfume reveals as united and any time it is inhaled one must separate it into its constitutive voices, evaluating its equilibrium and integrity, positivity and negativity. Take the perfume and contact it one time per each component note, feeling the notes split one by one and then combined together in the resultant perfume. Once seize fruit, then wood, and then test the development, the cleanliness, and the integrity. Let's nose and re-nose a thousand times the very same perfume so that its structure and shades will not have any more secrets.

Memories of the perfume: olfaction carries memories plenty of emotional sensations. What does this perfume remind me, where did I smell it, which wine had it and how was its perfume different from this one?

THE FLAVOUR OF WINE

With a lot of attention perceive this and even more of the taste of wine.

The flavour of wine: it is necessary to feel the flavour of wine and evaluate its equilibrium between sweetness, bitterness and acidity. Its pleasantness and the harmony of quality and quantity of diverse components, the constitutive voices of flavour, its single and diverse strengths. Different thrusts and counterthrusts, convergences and edges of diverse veins. Remember that flavour is the sensorial reverberation of the constituents of wine. Try to feel the acid sword, the bitter tail and the soft mass. Timber and harmonic multidimensionality of taste. Let's feel wine acidity while in the mouth, bitterness when wine is swallowed, softness around one or the other. Everywhere. Feel the freshness of its flavour, its partial or clean evolution, and its warmth from the contact given by its alcoholic degree. And finally while swallowing feel wine behaviour on the uvula, best revealer of non-integrity. The uvula must not be pinched by the sulphureous or pricked by the acetous: the state of rest of uvula is not changed by the passage of an integral wine as it happens with water, pure at maximum grade.

The touch of wine: wine must be felt inside mouth; it is necessary to feel its fibre, if watery or narrow, thick or liquid. Feel its extractive weight, the density or its fluent contact with lingual papilla. The all of this is the touch of wine, the most precise revealer of consistency.

In order to feel its touch and flavour, move wine inside the mouth and make wine touch the main part of receptive probes therein because any different visited zone gives the taste completeness and mutability.

Let's appreciate this with eyes shut; through a lot of small sips, one for each kind of examination. Notice with attention the result of each micro-analysis: think of it.

In the end, joining the three phases we shall discover that the perfume is the olfactory dress of the flavour.

The flavour is the gustative dress of the perfume.

The glance is the visual dress of the perfume and the taste.

EXAMPLES OF VALUATIONAL AND DESCRIPTIVE SCHEDULES

Taken from *Annuario dei Migliori Vini Italiani 2001*, the following are descriptive schedules of three among most pleasant Italian wines recently evaluated. Let's derive from them an example of the extreme expressive freedom, which can and must be exercised in describing sensations.

Idem Bianco Feudi di San Gregorio 1998 99

Consistency: 33 - Equilibrium: 33 - Integrity: 33

Sensations: ***you make your best to persuade men to be better, to be more logical. You talk of visions, of sensations predicted but not yet actualised as new and more positive aims. You aspire to perfection aware of the tranquillising distance from it. You deeply believe in what you are aiming to and you are very attentive to put the stakes very high so that maximum attainment becomes the most improbable, so that you cannot but always improve. With this kind of a tension towards the fruit – the first, perfect and imperfective fruit – 30.000 wines were been tasted. Then the imponderable: the encounter with this wine. The perception of its smell and flavour, credible only because testable. Here then a regret which in fact is perfect joy: despite everything had been said during all these years to narrate the gifts of the fruit, despite the most audacious interpolations of smells and flavours to prefigure to me the perfect wine-fruit, the nature, the reality was further on. With this wine now, the entire wine field is further ahead. Materialisation of the wine-fruit in a glass that moving my sensibility - never before moved this pleasantly – stupefies myself with a fantastic emotion: the certainty that for the entire wine field a new stately expressive register was open. Affected, I think to the many men who in past times had in mind the idea of producing a wine with such a good taste, and being less fortunate than we are not having technical capacity of reaching it. Moved, I pay homage to the human and professional talents belonging to those who succeeded in realising this wine. I place my glass on the table. I close the tasting session. It is not possible to drink anything else enjoying it after the tasting of this Italian champion. Any other wine is dumb in comparison with this new reference archetype among the white wines.***

We are on another planet: the planet of Pineapple Fruit.

P.S. the only sensation of this wine worth being described is the effect of the deep inhalation of its magic olfact: the elliptical spinning of the inspired perfumes in ascendant concentric circles streaming, lined and feathered by a fruit of absolutely unusual softness and freshness. Thanks to the exhaustive richness in extractive substances of the wine from which it is sent forth, this olfaction seems never to stop in bringing the fruitiness to my nostrils and pleasantness to the senses.

Type of wine: *White* – Price: *C* – Bottles: *6660* – First year of production: *1998* – Grapes: *Fiano, Greco, Moscato, Falanghina, Coda di Volpe, others* – Commune/vineyard: *Candida (Av)* – Name and vineyard surface: *Pian delle Vigne 22 he* – Exposure and altimetry: *south-west 500 m. on sea level* – Type of ground: *marly, arenaceous and calcareous rocks* – Culture system and vine density: *Guyot 4.000 plants/he* – Average vine age: *7/8 years* – Deduced grapes yield and yield per stool: *60 q., 1,5 Kg.* – Period of grape harvest: *end of October* – Fermentation tank: *wood* – Duration: *12 days* – Temperature: *18° degrees centigrade* – Temperature control: *yes* – Control system: *refrigerated interspaces* – Malolactic fermentation: *yes, total* – Steel/wood: *wood* – Type of wood: *oak* - Capacity: *50 hl and barriques 228 l.* – Age: *new* – Refinement: *yes* – Duration: *3 months* – Product stabilisation: *tartaric.*

Pafoj Rosso Icardi 1998 — *96*

Consistency: 33 - Equilibrium: 32 - Integrity: 31

Sensations: ***extreme the transparent pleasantness of this perfume. There is a magnificent alcohol, opening in sweetness the picture of smells and accompanying in depth each inhalant excursion. The power of alcohol degree corroborates energetically any effluvium inspired from the wine disk. It is possible to smell a very suasive blackberry fruit, striated with vanilla and mint. An alcoholic and crystalline transparency is felt on the strawberry lawn so pleasant - smelling – to be seen. Olfactory verse is all sweetness, caressing and souplesse. This great burden of aroma and perfumes is not loose; it is brought with algidity by the distilling alcoholic vector. It seems wine is not in the mouth so soft the caress of its flavour is. One is simply charmed by the density and the softness of the contact. The very rich extracts make wine move slowly like a slow motion effect introducing another kind of slowness also given by the exceptional supply of the extracts: the never ending persistency, during deglutition, of the strawberry-raspberry/mint-vanilla mix of the very balanced and sprinkling spicy thread. Nothing is bitter, rustic or old in this Piedmontese Red, the best tasted so far. A source of pride for our oenology, thanks to its delicate, algid, minty, raspberry fruit flavour. Perhaps so far only La Turque of Guigal gave a fruit this fleshy, alcoholic and ripe, but never a raspberry this clean and fresh. What a fabulous wine, which splendid perfumes. I had never met before a wine from such a good Nebbiolo.***

Type of wine: *Red* – Price: *D* – Bottles: *3500* – First year of production: *1997* – Grapes: *Nebbiolo* – Commune/vineyard: *Neive and Treiso* – Name and vineyard surface: *Starderi and Bricco Ausario 2 he* – Exposure and altimetry: *south-west, south-east 280 m. on sea level* – Type of ground: *calcareous marls* – Culture system and vine density: *Guyot 3.200 plants/he* – Average vine age: *40 years* – Deduced grapes yield and yield per stool: *70 q., 2,19 Kg.* – Period of grape harvest: *October* – Fermentation tank: *inox* – Duration: *10 days* – Temperature: *33° degrees centigrade* – Temperature control: *no* – Malolactic fermentation: *yes* – Total/Partial: *total* – Steel/wood: *wood* – Type of wood: *French oak* - Capacity: *225 l.* – Age: *everything new* – Refinement: *yes* – Duration: *6 months* – Product stabilisation: *filtration.*

Picolit Aquila del Torre 1997 95

Consistency: 33 - Equilibrium: 33 - Integrity: 29

Sensations: ***the pleasantness of this wine is fantastic. The simply exceptional richness and the consistency render the contact wine-tongue an extremely rare experience of viscosity and density. In this case the passage from the solid to the liquid phase, the transformation from fruit to wine has taken place with a dilution scale near to zero. A very sweet oil but never mawkish. The duty of balancing and controlling such an important mass of sugars belongs to a perfectly modulated acidity; to gustative spores of a bitter trend capable of rendering the very abundant and continuous pouring out of sweetness an experience always more and more pleasant. The ripeness and the juiciness of the used fruit are simply outstanding. Difficult to resist this wine: the number of its carats and aromatic complexity is not behind or at the same level, they decidedly exceed the organoleptic memories of the best Sauternes thickness and sweetness. The overtaking is brilliant not only in the equilibrium of the taste but also in the parameter of integrity which is technically the most difficult to be optimised, especially at this levels of consistency. Wine colour is blond, not dark and this means that taste-aroma is nor sugary nor rancid: the cleanliness is almost perfect. The wood, the spicy touch which softens mango, banana and tropical papaya – all minty, perfectly minty - with vanilla and saffron: an exquisite wine-fruit, oenologically perfectly made. The best Picolit ever tasted. A wine the taste of which lasts hours in the mouth and years in the mind of any wine lover. The white Italian Yquem is born. Honour and long life to this magic achievement.***

Type of wine: *Sweet* – Price: *D* – Bottle volume: *0,5 l.* - Bottles: *900* – First year of production: *1997* – Grapes: *Picolit* – Commune/vineyard: *Povoletto* – Name and vineyard surface: *Balarin-Pecol 0,6 he* – Exposure and altimetry: *south-east 230 m. on sea level* – Type of ground: *calcareous, marls* – Culture system and vine density: *modified Silvoz 2.500 plants/he* – Average vine age: *40 years* – Deduced grapes yield and yield per stool: *8,5 q., 0,34 Kg.* – Period of grape harvest: *half of October and about 2 months of withering* – Fermentation tank: *100% wood barriques* – Duration: *4 months* – Temperature: *20° degrees centigrade* – Temperature control: *yes* – Malolactic fermentation: *yes* – Total/Partial: *total* – Steel/wood: *wood* – Type of wood: *Allier and Limosine oak* - Capacity: *225 l.* – Age: *new* – Refinement: *yes* – Duration: *7 months* – Product stabilisation: *clarification and filtration.*

CHAPTER II

IMPORTANT ASPECTS FOR TASTING

THE SENSOR-MAN

In chemical ground with a sensor you can determine type and quantity of the substances contained in diverse material systems.

In nature sensor is man, capable of determining the nature and the intensity of everything he gets in touch with.

Our sensorial capability is enormous, always vivid and very sensitive, it also works without our consciousness: our detectors work even when we are sleeping. We always feel and in a very evident manner but only rarely – and without method or continuity - we carefully consider and evaluate what our sensor organs transduce out of the brain with a speed similar to the incoming one. In next paragraph I will focus on the importance of perceptive attention, here I would like to draw your attention to and let you appropriate of the following true concept: as a taster I am a *monster*. Why? Because we are made so as to result self-protected. Sensitivity = survival = capacity of self – preserving intact and unchanged in always better conditions. We feel well to live well.

This is why our eye is a magnificently versatile and perfect objective; this is why our nose is radar and sonar; this is why our mouth is an absolutely precise scale, capable of feeling micrometric variations of consistency and flavour.

I am talking about the dreadful sight capacity of our eye, of its faculty so innate in our existence of distinguishing colours infinitely shaded even ignoring that between two hues there might be 0,02 micron difference of wavelength only.

I am talking about the dreadful capacity of our nose to smell, of the faculty that invisible particles exercise when smelt by a man in a perfume:

the capability of recalling the memory of an emotion, of a feeling.
I am talking about the dreadful capacity of our mouth to register micrometric consistency and flavour variations inside it even caused by a simple hair: a trunk in a brook. Whichever thing any man was doing if he feels a hair in the mouth he would immediately stop to remove what his tongue would perceive as an enormous pole. And this would happen with a hair diameter of about a few microns of millimetre.
Therefore let no one ever doubt of the absolute extraordinariness of his sensorial capacities. Extraordinariness extraordinarily natural.
Therefore let no one ever say to himself "I am not able to feel to taste". It would be as saying "I am not able to breathe to live".

THE ATTENTION

Just like a radio that without aerial may transmit but cannot receive, without attention one may feel but could not perceive. Without perception the sensation is empty, it means nothing. Man is an itinerant sensorial receptor always on the ON position, always naturally and perfectly capable of registering sensations. But in order to have perception there must be attention.
Now you are reading my words with attention. This is why you do not perceive background noise, which surely is around you. Stop the reading, turn your attention from my lines to the background noise; you got it. In other words you have felt + thought of it. First you heard it but you did not perceive it.
Sensation without the perceptive attention is instinct. Sensation with no thought does not illustrate or explain what it transmits. It is not possible

to "earn" sensitivity, but it is possible to develop the capacity of perceiving. Sensitivity is a congenital factor not developable. In fact perceptiveness is infinitely developable: that is the capacity of understanding the result of sensations.

Let's close our eyes to think of what we perceived. Let's try to read with our thought what we have felt. Let's analyse in detail qualitative and quantitative result of each sensation and to do so let's repeat the sensations until we feel we have deeply understood it. In order to gaining perception capacity it is necessary to force and to repeat even one thousand time the sensation. One cannot say exactly how many times: sure all the times necessary to perceive more and more clearly and precisely what we are feeling. The receptor organ, for instance the nose, must be so tightly and directly – totally and continually - connected to the brain as to become brain itself. Inside our mind we must feel the perfume of a wine. And inside our brain we must feel the viscosity of wine touch. The element connecting the sensation to the perception, and eye - nose - mouth to the brain, is the attention. Without attention there exists no man capable of perceiving, in other words able of evaluating what he is feeling. Therefore there are not people unable to taste, to evaluate wine quality: simply there are people who, not analysing with attention what they feel, are unable to perceive sensorial quality of what they taste. And let's reflect on the difference between human beings and animals: animals with much stronger senses then ours but less gifted with wits; human beings "superior" because more capable of understanding what we feel in a less clear and strong manner. If so far you didn't pay attention to the sensations produced by diverse wines and foods; if from today you will begin evaluating attentively - thinking of the effects registered by your sensitivity when touched by a certain wine - you will be amazed by the clearness and the speed with which it is possible to perceive the quality of different wines. The object of the analysis, the wine, moves the senses interpreted by the brains. The attention must be the subject. Let's mentally appropriate of our capacity of feeling and exercise the perceptive consciousness of man's natural sensorial faculties: then also a dust micro-grain would be perceived by our sense as an enormous iceberg.

THE SINCERITY AND THE IMMEDIATENESS OF SENSATION

Any sensation even immediate is true in itself. Sensor organs are never wrong in reception and in transmission, but the intellectual perception of the sensation may be more or less frequently right or wrong. The less directly and attentively we think of what we felt, the wronger we can be in interpreting it. The first odour or the first flavour impression is the true one. We have to understand it and explain it, giving an evaluation of it. Let's evaluate wine quality on the basis of the sensations generated by the contact with wine and not evaluate the quality on the basis of abstract ideas. The more sincerely we will answer for what is registered by our senses, the more precious and valuable we will be as tasters, as sensorial analysts.

RELATION WINE-TASTER: HOW SENSORIAL ANALYSIS WORKS

To the taster's senses wine results as per its chemical and physical composition. As the taste of any gastronomic preparation rely on the quality and the quantity of the ingredients, wine taste depends on the quality and the quantity of its components.

Therefore tasting is an organoleptic examination (through sensor organs eye, nose and mouth) of an actual analytical reality (the whole of wine components).

The chemical-physical wine component, for instance sugar, provokes a stimulus which, received by the sensor organ (eye, nose and mouth), reflects the sensation then interpreted and perceived by the brain as sweetness. The wine components are the agents of the sensations. A simple cause-effect relation.

I understood and experimented this at the beginning of my profession, when I asked myself "how does tasting work? The variation of what inside wine determines the variation of the way wine results to the senses? Which is the relation between wine and taster?" Immediate and logical the answer.

Wine is a whole of chemical-physical compounds: each one of them and the whole of them cause a sensorial stimulation. The sensations perceived by the taster while tasting are the effect of such stimulation. The organoleptic performance of any wine depends on its chemical composition (see pic. 1).

But then if this is true and if this is always true, it is possible to scientifically study the relation between the chemical wine composition and its sensorial performance, so as to single out the constituent profile of wine: what determines the organoleptic quality and the pleasantness and what determines non-quality and unpleasantness.

WINE		TASTER
WHOLE OF CHEMICAL-PHYSICAL COMPOUNDS ↓ CAUSE OR AGENT	→	SENSATION ↑ EFFECT
TANNIN	→	BITTER
SULPHURED HYDROGEN	→	SULPHUREOUS
CHEMICAL-PHYSICAL WINE COMPOSITION	→	SENSORIAL PERFORMANCE

Picture 1

So I established a new branch in wine tasting: the sensorial-chemical analysis. I used to buy 2 bottles of a certain wine. I tasted the first writing a descriptive schedule and the wine evaluation in hundredths; the second was sent to a laboratory from which I was given the analytical profile with titration of the 21 chemical and constituent parameter macro-parameters. On a page of my technical magazine, in a column created for this purpose entitled "Survey: sensorial-chemical analysis", I published first the evaluation schedule, then the chemical profile and in the end I discussed the sensorial performance, knowing its chemical profile. Helped by Prof. Aldo Fioravanti, after 5 years of study and research and after having subjected more than 200 wines to this sensorial analysis, I succeeded in determining in a formula the chemical structure of the wine pleasantness. Now the analytical profiles any wine must possess to result pleasant is well known, and vice versa. Likewise, the chemical physical agent of each perceived sensation, good or bad, is well known. And well known is also the variation of any sensation at the qualitative and quantitative variation of the chemical physical originating agent and of the other wine components. Knowledge that when applied to wine production, through an aimed viticultural and oenological development, allows the technical reproducibility of a certain Index of Pleasantness, thus obtaining wines systematically and no more accidentally pleasant.

THE WILL OF TASTING

Tasting is different from drinking. The taster is not a drunkard. Tasting means to determine the Index of Quality – Pleasantness – Fruitiness of an examined wine. This, through measuring the intensity of the three qualitative parameters which decides it (Consistency, Equilibrium, Integrity). Tasting does not mean drinking wine in order to appreciate its pleasant and stirring effects. The taster is sober because he knows that his full mental presence is fundamental for tasting. A great attention is necessary for the full thinking and understanding what our senses register when they get in touch with a wine. In order to taste you have to desire it: you must have the will to relate to wine in a technical and attentive manner, not in a convivial way. And to relate with a wine which offers a stock of stimulation and also with who is approaching to this subject between hedonism and technicality. The very same option you have in front of a written page: if to quickly glance over it or attentively read it.

THE TASTER'S ATTITUDE

Said it all about the will of tasting, basic factor for a technical and fair trim towards the glass, the taster must keep in mind the following inspir-

ing criteria in order to do well.
When tasting one is more animal than human being. You do not have to worry about how you look while tasting; in fact all you have to think of is to feel as more as possible. Sometimes, when I lead tasting sessions in public I ask people if a certain smell is perceived, a particular sensorial datum of the examined wine. The participants timidly bring their nose nearer to the glass, inspiring air keeping the face at more than 10 centimetres from the crystal. No! Nose must be inside glass, possibly bending on one side, so as to offer the odorous stream a wider surface of the mucosa sensitive to the perfumes. The nose tip must nearly touch the wine disk, inspiration must be deep, repeated as many times as necessary, the eyes shut when you are thinking of what nose and palate are feeling, perceiving through this the nature and the intensity of the odorous and gustative flow. You have to feel. Each part of our body must aim to this with the total participation of the organism and the intellective faculties to perception. The right spirit is the one of a challenge. Examined wine is my enemy until I identify its Consistency, Equilibrium, and Integrity: its Index of Quality-Pleasantness. And you cannot joke with the enemy: you deeply study it, you burn it, you consume it with your nose and palate until you completely adhere to its nature, until you permeate each other. If deciding to envelop some cheese in a transparent plastic film I let film adhere to cheese as more precisely as possible, without even the smallest wrinkle between the wrapping and the content, it will be impossible to see the film: it has become a piece of cheese itself. This is how the taster must adhere to wine, adhere to the wine nature up to become wine himself. It is necessary to smear yourself on the wine and then to subside leaving no traces. The taster is a scale and a reporter: he weighs with top pre-

cision the intensity of the three parameters determining the Pleasantness of examined wine and then renders as faithfully as possible the sensations registered during the sensorial contact with wine.

THE SENSATIONS: ANALYSIS AND TIME OF ANALYSIS

In no one of the many books I read before becoming wine writer there was any indication on the nature and the perception of sensations. Sensation is immaterial: this is why it is difficult to think and talk of it and describe it. No matter originating from matter, something that if felt can also be studied and illustrated. Being transient and volatile it needs great attention to be caught and great insistence to be known first, then recognised and judged. Do not fear to begin studying sensations registered while getting in touch with wine. Just as no one of us would find it difficult to describe a colour, in the very same way, with our own words and thoughts, let's describe the perfume and the flavour we feel while tasting a wine. Be humble, do not fear asking anything to anyone, to compare with others. Just be as true as possible, concentrated and methodical. Begin with asking yourself the most banal questions on sensations – here banal means essential. What kind of a nature does this perfume have? Is it acid, bitter, soft; is it clean, thick, and fresh. What does it remind me of? When did I smell it before? What kind of intensity does it have? Inhale this perfume from the glass as many times are necessary to feel and understand more. There is no time limit. While tasting time is not a qualitative factor. Let everyone simply get all time necessary to evaluate with best possible precision the intensity and the nature of the qualitative parameters, of the shades, of the comprehensive nature of the examined wine. Keep in mind that the longer and the more attentive the study is, the more precise the evaluation, the more definite and indelible the memorisation will be. And the more expert and skilled as sensorial analyst the taster will be.

ENVIRONMENT AND ENVIRONMENTAL ARRANGEMENT

Where and how a tasting session takes place influence the results of tasting as no other factor. Naturally inexperienced, at the beginning of my activity I used to technically taste in the most diverse ways (without a true method) and in the most different places. So it happened that *X* wine tasted in *Z* place under *Y* conditions resulted to my senses different from it seemed if tasted in *W* place under *K* conditions. The same Barolo tasted soft and harmonic in producer's cellar, acid and tannic in a restaurant, short and alcoholic in the house of some friends. So I understood that to become reliable as a taster, in order to measure with precision the quality of so many wines, I had to use the same method and I had to taste as much as possible in the same environment. So, the very same wine ended up with revealing differently, but reproposing on second, third and on any subsequent tasting the Consistency, the Equilibrium and the Integrity shown during the first. Therefore if many different wines are tasted always in the same place and in the same environmental conditions the only thing which changes from one tasting to the others is wine. Substance variations can be better recognised if the shape with which they appear is identical.

THE COMPARISON

In order to evaluate the intensity of the three parameters determining the wine Quality-Pleasantness it is important to simultaneously compare more than 1 wine. A sample that in absolute terms could be defined as rich, if compared to a thicker can result fluid; one which seems balanced in absolute terms, compared to another even more harmonic can reveal acid; one that seems clean can result perturbed with reference to another more integral. Primarily the comparing more wines during the same tasting is necessary in order to perceive with substantial truthfulness the intensity of the three parameters determining their quality (to compare wines is absolutely useful to evaluate with precision – through comparison – the intensity of their Consistency, Equilibrium and Integrity). Secondarily it is useful to identify with precision a sort of wine prototype chiefly consistent, balanced and integral with which to compare all the other tasted wines. You can measure the Consistency of examined wine comparing it with the one of the richest wine you are tasting, or comparing it to the (memorised) one of the most consistent wine evaluated in the past. A model, a sort of archetype the less approximate possible that can be fixed with precision only after several compared tastings.

THE ORGANOLEPTIC MEMORY

From what written above, a taster is the more reliable the wider and the more definite his organoleptic memory is. The more numerous are the diverse memorised levels of consistency, equilibrium and integrity, the more precise is the evaluation of the intensity of the three parameters of tasted wines. So in order to develop a good organoleptic memory the comparison is useful and the method fundamental. If any time I taste I evaluate a different aspect in a different way, I will remember nothing of the many tasted wines. It is impossible to memorise inhomogeneous comparisons; the method instead promotes the memorisation of the characteristics of several wines analogously tasted.

USEFUL DEVICES FOR GOOD TASTING

1) Tasting must be performed with the taster always seated on the same chair, in the same position with reference to environment; the identity of place and positioning exalts the perceptivity of what changes (wine inside glass) and renders homogeneously memorisable what senses register.
2) The top of the tasting table must be white thus to favour and not to alter colour analysis.
3) The light conditions of the tasting place must always be the same; wine must be strongly illuminated, it is excellent a lamp with 100-watt bulb addressed on the white top of the shelf for glasses. Almost total darkness around. The attention necessary to register sensations produced by wine is matured and kept longer in a dark place; if everything that is out of our cone of attention is in the dark, we can focus our attention only on what is illuminated.
4) One is more attentive and concentrated if alone. While tasting in public let's concentrate all the time necessary to measure the intensity of the three parameters determining wine quality. Everywhere and anyway it is possible to go in depth with our own attention: it is a matter of will, concentration, training.

5) It is better to taste on empty stomach and with clean mouth. If you haven't been eating for about 1 hour, saliva tends to re-establish its neutrality. Mouth and saliva better register the flavours and the contact viscosity if devoid of any residual taste-aromatic persistence determined by recent consumption of food and drinks. This is why it is damaging to interpose tasted wines with solid food of any consistency or flavour: not only do scums have their own taste thus modifying the manifestation and the perception of the Equilibrium, but they also interferes with the manifestation and the perception of wine Consistency.
6) It is useful to give tasting a circadian rhythm. Also the senses feel time. If we get used to taste on a certain time of the day, at that time our sensorial apparatus will become particularly sensitive. In the very same way the hanger stimulus works: lunchtime and dinnertime we have more appetite.
7) Used glasses must always be identical, rigorously in glass or plain crystal (see pic. 2: I.N.A.O. or I.S.O. are optimal).
8) Filling up level must absolutely be identical in any glass. The more wine is in the glass, the more coloured and perfumed it will be. A glass fuller of a wine less coloured and perfumed can result more coloured and perfumed than a second glass less full of a more coloured and perfumed wine.

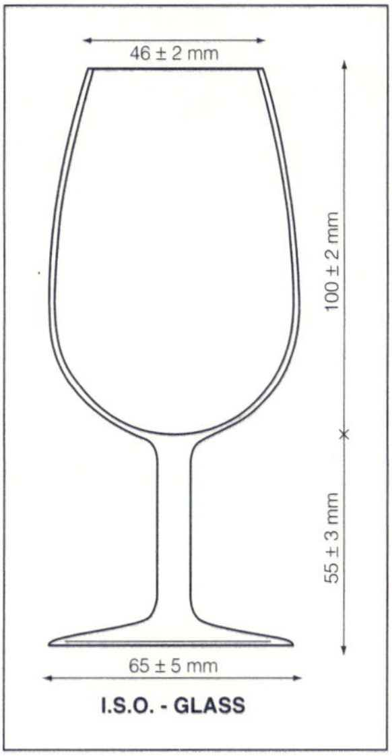

Picture 2

9) No soap or detergent rests must be present inside glasses (they can contaminate wine taste-aroma).
10) Taster's hands must not be very perfumed.
11) All tasted wines must have the same temperature. Because a) the same wine but colder results more consistent to the touch (yoghurt in the fridge becomes denser, hot oil is fluider). b) The cold renders perfumes and aromas less perceivable (cork defect is almost unperceivable if wine is cooled to freezer temperature). The best tasting would be at ambient temperature. The average temperature of places in which a technical wine tasting can take place varies from 18 to 27 degrees centigrade: these thermic values do not alter or damage organoleptic characteristics. Besides, a wine refrigerated at pleasure tends very quickly to return to ambient temperature so it is oppor-

tune to taste it at a temperature similar to the one at it would be tasted by everyone.

12) The number of the anonymous tasted samples should be constant; it may anyway vary from a minimum of two to a variable maximum depending on the taster's experience and the desired accuracy of the analysis. It is good to proceed with two wines to let the fundamental qualitative comparison of the registered sensations take place. But no more than twenty as maximum number because I think this is the limit in evaluating samples without intellectual tiredness or sensorial weariness. In any case it is advisable a number which should be proportionate to the taster's training in order to have the same homogenous concentration conditions from the first to the last tasting.
13) The taster must have paper and pen or a PC in order to note the registered sensations, describe the organoleptical profiles of wine, express his own judgement (even quantitative) on the sensorial qualities of tasted sample. To write it is necessary to reflect and pay attention, just as it must be done for well tasting. The construction and the progressive increase of our organoleptic memory are facilitated by noting the results of different tastings on a notebook or on apposite schedules. In fact through writing the results of our observations we gradually improve our valuational and descriptive capacities.
14) The olfaction gets tired and quickly becomes accustomed: in order to regain sensitivity to nostrils it is useful to subject to technical olfaction an I.S.O. glass full of water. Through the smelling of nothing (inspiring from water air with no perfume) olfactory channels regain sensitivity. Going back to wine after smelling water, the perfume we could not catch beforehand will result very clear.

TO RECOGNISE WINES

The function of tasting is to establish the Index of Quality-Pleasantness of a wine through a scrupulous examination and a description of the registered sensations. The belief that a good taster is the one who is able to recognise year, wine and producer name of an anonymous sample is totally false. Recognisability is not a value and who concentrates on identifying wines is a very bad taster, unable (because not interested) to evaluate the intimate qualitative essence of a wine (Consistency, Equilibrium and Integrity of its taste).

THE INUREMENT TO SENSATIONS

In interpreting a specific gustative note (positive or negative) palate tiredness and inurement phenomena must be considered: a feeble answer from the receptor to an identically repeating stimulation. The taste, as the olfaction, gets immediately used to a certain sensation, unable of perceiving for a long time the same taste or the same smell, even if strong. For instance, people get used to their perfume and they do not seize any more its intensity or superimposition; entering a garage one can immediately smell a strong petrol scent which is no more perceived after a few minutes. This is why due to the regular drinking of defective wines one cannot recognise the defect. A vice which becomes normality, or even a merit, due to the frequency with which it occurs (peasants judge their imprecise wines very good because they drink good wines very seldom). Some people think that negative smells perceived at the beginning of the tasting with time eventually weaken or disappear: very wrong. For what we have said so far, when a defective wine is tasted, the defect clearly results in its nature and intensity from the first olfaction or sip. Afterwards, due to the inurement that attenuates the perception almost to cancellation, the defect seems disappeared and wine becomes nearly acceptable. In reality the defect is always there and to entirely appreciate it is sufficient to approach that wine after a few minutes, or it is enough to compare that wine to a clean one. Vice interference will be identical, its negative influence absolutely equal to itself.

THE DESCRIPTION AND THE ANALOGIES OF A WINE

In order to describe a wine it is not necessary to use abstruse terms: it is sufficient to describe nature and intensity of registered sensations. This is to be done in the manner and using the language each taster would feel as the most natural and the best possible. A heartfelt schedule is a well-done schedule. As far as analogies stimulated by wine perfume or taste are concerned, it is ridiculous and useless trying to seek for peculiar analogies proposed by a wine. Who describes a wine only listing the strangest evoked perfumes shows himself as a non-reliable taster. Let's describe first the Consistency, then the Equilibrium and the Integrity of a wine: in practical terms its capacity of resulting pleasant at the taste. Then, secondarily, the eventual presence of complementary analogic recalls nearby the constitutive fruit, the grape (similarity among perfumes and/or taste of a wine and perfumes and/or taste of another known fruit). The analogy is important – and can be quoted – only if proposed in a very evident manner by the wine itself as an immediate recollection, easily received and identified by any taster, not only by the professional one. If drawing the nose near the glass the wine perfume imposes us to state "this is apricot", then on its evaluation schedule we can-must note that this wine recalls this fruit. Such a pregnant note as to be felt by each and everyone and immediately recognised. The good taster slogan is "I write as per I taste". The image more valuable to portray the deductivity of a good taster's descriptive action is the following: wine bears the pen of who is describing it.

THE VINTAGE

Vintage determines the quality of fruit. It is worth a projection of 50% of product value. The cellar determines the remaining 50%. A good year is necessary but not sufficient a condition to obtain a wine with high Index of Quality. It is certain that with equal transformation capacities (oenological capacities) the better is the season, the better is harvested fruit and the better is produced wine. Besides this, we have to consider that also the quality of operators determines the influence of the vintage parameter. A skilled vinedresser will harvest at an optimal ripening index a consistent fruit. One less skilled will compromise good seasonal result with inadequate and/or untimely interventions; he will harvest at a non-optimal maturation point unhealthy grape lacking in consistency. A proficient oenologist will succeed in transmitting the organoleptical characteristics of the constitutive fruits (without filters or distortions) untouched into the wine. A less skilled one will compromise with inadequate and/or untimely interventions the original sensorial patrimony of fruits obtaining a mediocre wine, not resembling at all the organoleptic characteristics of the harvested grape. Therefore the influence of parameter vintage is proportional to producer's technical qualities.

As per what we have said great years can give small wines and great wines can come up from average or mediocre years. So never buy a wine before having tasted it. Equation great vintage of great producer = good wine is seldom satisfied and this is why it is always necessary to taste a sample of wine before stocking it in our own cellar.

WINES AND WOOD

Wine passage in wood during production can: 1) gift the wine taste-aroma spectre with an additional dimension, accompanying fruit notes with those of spices, mint, exotic and suasive balms just as soft and sweet. 2) Distort the fruit taste-aroma, superimposing extraneous notes having nothing to do with former sweetness of ripe grape: caramel, cooked vegetables, tar. Hypothesis 1) is that of a wine revealing during tasting the primary fruit, very limpid and rich of its own aromas, increased by a bonus of minty and balsamic scents derived from oak. In other words an amount of positive perfumes adding to the already positive ones properly deriving from grape: a fruit raised to the spices. Hypothesis 2) is that of a wine not giving any fruit scent but only a smell whose root is the fruit but whose product is something dark, bitter, acetous and ligneous: the grape transfiguration.

In any case in order to realise first hypothesis (increase of sweetness volume) the barrels must be recent – better if brand new, anyway not contaminated. It is also necessary that the rest in wood is not too long in order to avoid the oxidation of wine and of the aroma released by the wood. The second hypothesis (transfigured fruit) takes place when the wood of maturation barrels is old and hygienically unhealthy. If a producer does not have healthy barrels what is the point of placing wine in old ones? Why loosing

fruit? It would be better to preserve the fruit and its freshness immediately placing wine in steel tanks or - even better - in glass bottles.
During the production the long rest of wine in wood originates from two factors: first of all in the past no alternative materials to contain wine existed (steel, glass, fibreglass, etc.). Secondarily due to lack of technology, wine could only be stabilised by a long stay in wood (with various precipitations of constituent substances determined by the thermic variation of seasons following one another). Nowadays it is possible to stabilise wine in many other manners, cellar tanks are realised in so many different materials: thus the passage in wood is operated uniquely to acquire an additional fraction of spicy aromas. Today the wood is the only permitted aromatisation.
As far as the wood released sweetness bonus is concerned we must consider that too long a stay in barriques or in big barrels can anyway imply a cost in terms of total quality-pleasantness. In fact wood can 1) penalise the wine integrity reducing its cleanliness due to the volatile acidity increase (agent of acetous sensation vs. fruit). 2) Penalise the wine integrity reducing its newness by the oxidation increase. 3) Penalise the taste equilibrium due to the bitter and rancid taste of the transferred aromatic substances (vanillic acid = oak tannate) and/or of the promoted oxidation. 4) Reduce the potential wine longevity due to the promoted oxidation (the wines aged for long times do not grow old for long). After all it is necessary to draw the spices - very soon ceased - from wood and to avoid the volatile increase, the oxidations, the duskings and caramelising, the acidifications and mainly the bittering of wine taste, defects which can irreversibly be caused by a clumsy wood usage. Let's remember that the fruit and not the wood gives the quality of wine.

IMPORTANT SUGGESTIONS FOR THE LOVER – CONSUMER – TASTER

1) If it is the result of an attentive and methodical analysis it is always better to follow one's own organoleptic judgement than someone else's. What is felt is truer than anything else, never doubt of our sensorial faculties. Never renounce our sensorial evaluation favouring another one based on abstract extra-sensorial ideas. Look at the children and try to say a child that food X – unpleasantly tasting and therefore disdainfully refused – is superior quality because rare, expensive, produced in few samples, on a particular year, result of secular traditions and/or of vanguard productive processes. Never would the child – perfect taster because sensorially pure – abandon, modify, retreat his judgement naturally based upon the qualitative essence of every food: the pleasantness of its taste. His qualitative judgement on the tasted product will be moved higher only by a more pleasant taste.
2) With reference to all sensations registered during tasting, and in order to increase your capacities of wine reading, description, objective evaluation, it is always necessary to ask yourself (and always find an answer to this question) what is this sensation? Where does it come from and what does it produce?
3) Should lover realise he cannot taste a lot of wines by himself because lacking of time, stimulus or money, he could consider the opportunity to refer to a source (a guide or a specialised magazine) for the quality individuation and the eventual purchase of the many wines on the market.
4) Uncritically relying upon a source can produce a cellar full of bad wines. Before following a certain source it is necessary to essay its reli-

ability in actual fact. Thus a) find a wine described by the source you want to test; b) open up the bottle and pour wine into the glass; c) compare the source's description and evaluation to yours, through direct organoleptical analysis. Check inside the glass the plausibility of each observation accomplished by the source, likelihood of the total traced profile and the foundation of the attributed score. Repeat this examination for at least 5 wines. Repeat this examination random (the source is human, therefore subjected to unpredictable changes). After this kind of trial the lover can follow this source for purchase only if he finds confirmation of the source's statements inside glass.

5) Do not trust reported judgements as reliable or judgements derived by not technical tastings. Try not to be motivated in buying wine only by extemporaneous comments made by third parties or even by personal tastings performed in not technical circumstances or with not technical methods (at the restaurant, with the producer, during a sector fair, during a wine presentation, etc.). Therefore never buy a great quantity of a wine whichever fame the producer can have or the importance of the vintage may be without properly tasting beforehand at least a bottle, or without reading a detailed and positive review given by a proved reliable source.
6) Who is inside the glass and talks as per how he felt is strong and can easily argue his opinion. Who is not inside the glass and talks as per how he reads or thinks, either does not have organoleptic opinions or – if he has them – he cannot propose or prove them because unfounded.
7) To the person who will begin systematically practising the tasting discipline the tasting schedules will appear meagre and synthetic: only a few notes on the intensity of the fundamental organoleptic characters.

Along with experience increase they will get progressively more articulated and complex (not less true because of this): outline of the complementary organoleptic characters of examined wine and of the various registered shades. In the end with full and conscious acquisition of method the descriptive schedules of wines will get to a fair length.

8) At the beginning of practice it is better to blindly taste samples in order not to be conditioned. With time passing, loosing any interest on what is outside the glass, tasting blindly or with the bottle in front of us will be absolutely the same. The reading will be anyway deep and detailed, the judgement objective and reliable because we shall have experimented that the unique interesting investigation site, the only source of organoleptic knowledge is the glass of wine. When you know how to taste the only important thing is to evaluate with method the substantial objective quality of the examined wine. Besides any conditioning, this is the pleasure of true knowledge.

GOOD TASTER'S REQUISITES

After all to properly evaluate the Index of Pleasantness - Quality - Fruitiness of a wine it is necessary:

1) Will: you have to desire to give a technical analytical judgement on the Index of Quality-Pleasantness of the examined wine.
2) Method: if you taste without a method you cannot be analytical in surveying, precise in evaluation, you are not quick and cannot memorise what you perceive.
3) Applied knowledge of method – experience: the theoretical knowledge of the method is not enough and application practice is essential.

4) Attention: only will attentive a taster perceive and precisely evaluate what is registered by the sense organs.
5) Immediateness, sincerity, deductivity and pregnancy in evaluating and describing what he feels.

CHAPTER III

INSIDE THE GLASS: THEORY

QUALITY OF WINE: WHAT DOES IT CONSIST ON?

The quality of wine is the pleasantness of its taste, in other words its fruitiness.

The experience shows that wines recalling constitutive fruit - the grape - in their flavour are unanimously recognised during tasting as the best ones, the ones with better quality. Everyone likes them, with no exception and for these wines recollecting fruit no abstemious exists. No abstemiouses with the wine-fruit, since no abstemiouses with wines with high Index of Pleasantness.

After all: quality = pleasantness = fruitiness are synonymous terms.

Premise which becomes axiom.

Axiom*

Wine is pleasant when its taste
recalls in a true way (consistent, balanced and integral)
that of fruit from which it is obtained.

From here it comes that wanting to give a substantial judgement on the pleasantness of a wine, it is necessary to evaluate its fruitiness grade.

Logisma **of wine fruitiness**

The wine fruitiness is proportional to
the Consistency, the Equilibrium and the Integrity of its taste

**Axiom is a statement the truth of which cannot be proved because self-consistent.*

***Logisma is a statement logically deduced from an axiomatic premise.*

From here it can be deduced that for wine:

$$\textit{Quality} - \textit{Pleasantness} - \textit{Fruitiness} = \textit{Consistency} + \textit{Equilibrium} + \textit{Integrity}$$

$$Q - P - F = C + E + I$$

THE THREE ORGANOLEPTIC PARAMETERS DETERMINING THE QUALITY OF WINE

Three are the organoleptic parameters common to any wine and determining its quality – pleasantness – fruitiness:

1) Consistency
2) Equilibrium
3) Integrity

Let's illustrate the meaning of each of them.

Consistency

Consistency is the set of substances constituting wine, its extract (consistency = extract). A wine total dry extract is the entire set of its constitutive components, excepted water, alcohol and substances dispersed by heat. It is obtained submitting wine to evaporation and it corresponds to fixed residual weight measured in grams g/l (weight in grams per litre of the dried fine powder remaining if we boil wine for a long time in a saucepan).
The more is the consistency of used grape, the more is wine consistency (wine extract depends on grape extract). The more grape is produced by a vine, the less consistent will be the produced wine (and vice versa).

In order to obtain fruits (and therefore wines) very rich in extract, viticulturers should let vine bear only few bunches.
Given the quantity of finished lymph which any plant succeeds in secreting, given the quantity of this substance destined to the survival and nutrition of the vegetation, smaller is the quantity of grape bunches pendent from a plant, bigger is the lymph fraction (extract) which will be precipitated in each fruit. Not many bunches produced = rich fruit = rich wine = wine produced in less quantity but better quality wine.
In substance the consistency of a wine is a rare merit because expensive.

Important notes on consistency

1) Consistency determines quantity of perceived sensations, in other words the intensity of visual, olfactory and gustative sensations. The more consistent is a wine the richer it is in colour, perfume, taste, presenting a dense and viscous touch (vice versa for inconsistent wines). Consistency is the expressive volume of a wine. Just as the volume of an amplifier determines the strength and not the balance between high and low notes, nor sound cleanliness, in the very same way the consistency – in other words, the wine volume – determines the strength with which taste is expressed. If wine is not balanced, high consistency will clearly point out such a disharmony; if wine has a defect this will be strongly felt in a high consistency wine: the consistency helps if wine has good equilibrium and integrity otherwise it is a boomerang.
2) Consistency is a macro-parameter: persistency of wine taste and potential longevity are direct function of its consistency. In fact, as far as persistency is concerned the stronger is the taste of a wine, the longer its

aromatic farewell trail is. As far as potential longevity is concerned, the more is the quantity of constituent substance to degrade the longer wine lasts through time. The more a wine is rich in extract, the longer will be necessary to oxidise any particle it is made of.

3) Besides certain levels consistency generates the saturation of the sensations (diminishing wine drinkability): therefore consistency excesses or defects damage in the same way the pleasantness. Just as wines too poor in extracts – diluted wines - are less appreciated, wines too concentrated result gushy, too strong, difficult and/or unpleasant to drink.
4) The constitutive chemical-physical agent of consistency is net dried extract of wine (expressed in grams per litre). There are two possible measurements of dried extract: a) total dried extract = net dried extract (g/l) + residual sugars (g/l); b) net dried extract = total dried extract (g/l) – residual sugars (g/l). Between two wines having equal total dried extract, denser to touch it results the wine with higher net dried extract: the touch is given by net extract. Therefore consistency true indicator is the net extract. Between two wines with equal net dried extract, the wine with more quantity of residual sugars – with more total dried extract - is the denser to the touch.
5) Knowing the nature of the parameter, it is possible to address viticultural and oenological practises to obtaining high consistency wines. Producers have different options first in vineyard, secondarily in cellar, to obtain grapes, then wines, rich in extracts.

Equilibrium

A wine is balanced when its taste fulfils the fundamental equation of the gustative equilibrium:

Eq = Sweet Taste Substances = Acid Taste Substances + Bitter Taste Substances

Or

Eq = STS = ATS + BTS

A wine is balanced when the sweetness (softness) of its taste is equal to the sum of its acidity and eventual bitterness. It is not balanced when one of the three gustative sensations is predominant.

With reference to gustative sensations it might be observed that in all books studying the gustative characteristics of aliments, out of the acid, bitter or salty sensations only the unpleasantness is measured. Tasting a spoonful of salt, acid or quinine a great unpleasantness is perceived. In fact pleasantness felt tasting a sugar spoonful is enormous and this universally occurs. This is why sugar is quoted on the stock exchange, not the acid and never the bitter. The physiological reason why sugar generates pleasantness is deeply touching. The brain - superiorly developed in human species - feeds on sugar and this is why it is congenitally and genetically more in need of sugar than other living primates are. And which more natural invitation to sugar consumption than its sensorial linkage to the highest pleasantness? This is why nature works sweetly: to pleasantly nourish creatures living in it. Just as naturally miraculous is the reason why such an unpleasantness can be felt at the contact with acid or bitter tastes: in nature acid substances are toxic, the poisonous bitter. The determinant of pleasantness and unpleasantness is the species survival.

Especially unnatural to go against these laws.

As regards the function of gustative equilibrium wine taste can present in three different ways:

1) STS = ATS + BTS, the case of a balanced wine, with soft taste, harmonic, multivaried and multidimensional. An instant sweet, then acid and fairly bitter. Then here it comes the softness, the only complex taste besides pleasantness. A round taste, never equal to itself in a diverse moment: a rolling taste with no peaks.

2) STS > ATS + BTS, the case of sweet wines, not balanced but pleasant.

3) STS < ATS + BTS, the case of acid wines or acid-bitter wines more than soft and therefore unpleasant. In the first case acid wine will have a more or less dry and lemony taste, sour. In the second bitter wine will have the taste of rhubarb, liquorice, medicine, and chinaroot.

Acid or bitter wines: the genesis of the twelve millions abstemiouses today in Italy. Persons that due to the above discussed natural reasons do not find it as pleasant to drink a beverage more acid and bitter than soft. So the reason of scarce and decreasing wine consumption is not cultural but purely sensorial. Let's produce wines balanced in taste and abstemiouses will disappear. The Equilibrium of the taste is wine drinkability.

The Equilibrium of wine taste depends on the equilibrium of fruit taste, on its ripeness index and also on followed vinification procedures. Minor is the ripeness level of used fruit, the acider the taste of the obtained wine. The unriper the fruit, the sourer the wine. The more the quantity of grape produced by a vine the more difficult is the fruit ripening. Not many bunches produced = well-ripened fruit = wine rich in sweet substances = balanced wine and therefore pleasant. The more is the quantity of polyphenolic substances (tannins and anthocyans) diluted in wine, the more the bitterness of its taste. Too tannic a wine = wine too rich in bitter substances = not balanced a wine because extra-bitter and therefore unpleasant.

Equilibrium in a wine is a rare merit because risky (postponing grape harvest exposes to climate risk) and also expensive: to have a perfect maturation it is necessary to produce less bunches per plant.

Important notes on equilibrium

1) Equilibrium determines the quality of perceived sensations. What kind of a perfume and what taste does a wine have solely depends on quantitative balancing of the diverse wine components (besides proper or improper wine components, that is its integrity).
2) Equilibrium is a macro parameter: only does a wine with balanced taste generate complex olfactory and gustative sensations because harmonic. If there is not taste equilibrium there is monotonous (not complex) excess of sweet, acid and/or bitter sensation. Only the sweetness excess (sweet wines) generates pleasantness even without any taste-aromatic complexity.
3) The constituent chemical-physical agent of equilibrium for wines scarce in sugar residuals is wine pH (expressed in pure number). Wine pH is the index expressing real or sensorial force of its acidity of titration (Total Acidity expressed in g/l).
4) Wine pH is a vital solution stabiliser. Determined by the moment in which fruit is detached from plant and by following vinification procedures, wine pH doesn't change through time and it must never change on pain of total decay of wine organoleptical qualities. Wine

becomes totally Madeirised and it is totally decrepit when its original pH changes due to the complete destruction of the constituent substances. In order to have an absolutely stable wine pH through time, pH is naturally endowed with a protection system, a sort of buffer which damps eventual pH movement attempts. Each wine has a diverse buffer power, index of stability of its pH.

5) With equal net dried extract a wine with conveniently modulated acidity or with higher sugar residual results softer at the touch: acidity and alcoholic grade render wine touch less fat and this is why I use to call them organoleptic tensor-tighteners.
6) Knowing the nature of the parameter it is possible to address viticultural and oenological practises to obtaining high equilibrium wines. The operator has different options first in vineyard, secondarily in cellar, to obtain grapes, then wines, with balanced taste, or as soft as acid-bitter.

Integrity

Wine taste is integral when the flavour of the constituent fruit is perceived in its cleanliness and newness.

Wine cleanliness consists on the absence of taste-aromas not proper of the grape and/or of the correct oenological product of its transformation. Cleanliness somehow related to the idea of "purity" and "limpidness" as notes marking in nature the fruit at the moment of its detachment from the plant. A clean wine is a wine not revealing during tasting negative characters not present in constituent fruit, altering or distorting wine perfume and taste: sulphureous, acetous, milky, ligneous, vanished perfumes or tastes.

Wine newness consists on the absence of oxidised taste-aromas not present in grape just harvested: sugary, toasted, rancid, caramel, Madeira. In other words newness is in nature the fantastic freshness of the grape at the moment of its detachment from the plant. How new is the fruit contained in tasted wine? Is it fragrant or oxidised? And if it is not fresh, if it is oxidised, how much is it withered and/or perished, how old is it?

Wine integrity depends on fruit integrity. Mouldy fruit makes mouldy wine, oxidised fruit makes oxidised wine, and contaminated fruit contaminated wine.
Besides fruit integrity, wine integrity relies upon the quality of the fruit transformation into wine.

Being all wines natural derivatives of grape, the whole of them should naturally recollect this constituent fruit in perfume and taste with consistency and variable equilibrium. If such a recollection is not presented by tasted wine it is certainly because this wine is not integral: it has some vices or it is perished or oxidised. If a wine does not recall constituent fruit it means that the oenological transformation was not optimally conducted. Oenology is therefore the art of respect. The best oenologist is who succeeds in translating the entire and untouched fruit taste-aromatic potential into wine without any kind of dispersion or distortions. When an oenologist succeeds in respecting the constituent fruit to the point in which only the change of state – from solid to liquid – of its patrimony of aromas and flavour is allowed, integrity of a wine can get closer to perfection. The more painstaking and fast is the vinification process, the higher the integrity of the wine will be.

The Integrity of a wine is in substance a rare merit because rare in operators are diligence and simplicity.

Important notes on integrity

1) Integrity determines the quality of perceived sensations. What perfume and what taste does a wine have solely depends on proper or improper components of wine and on its freshness, as well as on the quantitative balancing of the diverse wine components, that is its equilibrium.
2) Integrity is a macro parameter: only a wine with an integral taste generates complex sensations because linear and fresh. Only a wine bottled not much or not oxidised at all has a good residual potential longevity.
3) On the one hand human sensitivity needs several grams per litre of any substance to feel superior consistency of a wine, on the other just few milligrams per litre of contaminating substances are enough to clearly and irreparably damage its perfume or taste. We are more sensitive towards displeasure than towards pleasure, reason why high integrity wine has a real merit.
4) Perfume and taste of contaminating agents is acid and/or bitter. Perfume and taste of substances with oxidised taste is rancid and bitter. Integrity vices worsen taste equilibrium reinforcing bitterness.
5) The more chemical composition of a wine is devoid of chemical-physical agents determining defects and/or oxidation, the higher its analytical-sensorial quality is.
6) Knowing the nature of the parameter, it is possible to address viticultural and oenological practises to obtaining high integrity wines.

Operator has different options first in vineyard, secondarily in cellar, to obtain grapes, then wines, with perfect integrity, that is to say devoid of cleanliness defects and not oxidised.

Integrity is determined by 2 factors:

a) Cleanliness: absence of unpleasant and defective perfumes and tastes not proper of constituent fruit. Principal defects of wines are:

I° sulphureous: sulphur taste-aromas which confer to nose piquant notes, rustic, smoked and similar to rotten eggs; the same for taste + a pinching tickle, rough during deglutition, with a persisting taste very bitter in the mouth; constituent chemical-physical agent of sulphureous is hydrogen sulphide (expressed in milligrams per litre).

II° acetous: acetous taste-aromas which confer to nose vibrant and cleaving notes thus provoking analogies with synthetic substances, enamels and paints (in red wine: resin notes); the same for the taste + pungent vibration, acetous and hot/cold during deglutition; constituent chemical-physical agent of acetous are acetic acid, that is volatile acidity, and ethyl acetate (the first expressed in grams per litre, the second in milligrams per litre).

III° milky: milky taste-aromas which confer to nose yoghurt and sour milk notes; the same for the taste + acidulous-pungent note during deglutition (in red wines due to more or less tannic and oxidised substratum the analogy recalls milk toffee); constituent chemical-physical agent of milky is diacetyl (expressed in milligrams per litre).

IV° vanished: dull and sweetish taste-aromas which confer to nose olive and wax notes; the same for the taste + brassy flavour (vanished is the perfume of a wine opened the day before); constituent chemical-physical agent of the vanished is acetic aldehyde (expressed in milligrams per litre).

V° ligneous: too much spicy and toasted taste-aromas derived from too long a stay in wood barrels. To the nose over-wood generates unnatural analogies with vanilla, spices, smoked, lake, copal; the same for the taste + bitter note during deglutition; constituent chemical-physical agent of the ligneous is vanillic acid (expressed in milligrams per litre).

b) Newness: absence of oxidation. Oxidation is the degradation of the original perfumes and tastes of the fruit due to improper vinification procedures and/or due to excessive wine ageing. Constituent chemical-physical agent of oxidation is esters (expressed in grams per litre).

Three are the progressive phases of oxidation

I phase: alteration and increase of reflection intensity and chromatic charge (in white wines accentuation of golden tones, in red wines appearance of orange tints). Loading of sweet and caramel notes to nose and taste: wine results sugary, gushy, soapy, sweetish, and weak (not sweet), toasted with first sign of rancid.

II phase: growing rank; at the eye white wines present a hue darkening, red wines turn to brick red. At the nose in white wines rancid appears through recollections to macaroon, almond, rancid butter; in reds caramel advances; the same for the taste + bitter note of old wines for whites, for reds caramel together with the bitterish of rancid.

III phase: Madeirisation. At the sight for white wines hue darkening, in reds colour is completely orange/garnet red; at the nose and taste there is no more freshness and notes become the oxidised ones belonging to Madeira. A metallic taste, like rusty, with sweetish and bitter taste after deglutition.

GENERAL CONSIDERATIONS ON THE THREE PARAMETERS DETERMINING THE QUALITY OF WINE

1) The three parameters determining wine quality are not purely theoretical but analytically measurable (through titration in laboratory of related constituent chemical-physical agents)
2) Each one of the three parameters concurs in identical manner (33,33%) to the determination of the absolute quality – pleasantness – fruitiness of any wine.
3) None of the three parameters determines on it's own the quality – pleasantness – fruitiness of a wine. A wine is a quality wine and has a high Index of Pleasantness if at the meantime it is very consistent, balanced and integral.
4) None of the three parameters determines on it's own the unpleasantness, non-quality, and non-fruitiness of a wine. A wine has a very low Index of Pleasantness if at the meantime it is not much consistent, balanced and integral.
5) The level of each fundamental organoleptical parameter is fixed once and for all by the producer through wine bottling.
6) Among themselves the three fundamental parameters are independent in proportioning but they interact in sensorial revelation. Because: a) the more consistent is a wine, the more it is possible to appreciate the

equilibrium or non-equilibrium of its taste. The same must be said for the perceptibility of a defect or a certain oxidation stage of a wine: the higher is the expressive volume of a wine – direct function of its consistency -, the more relevant its vice and/or its oxidative decay result. b) The more a wine is balanced and round at taste, the softer and thicker (not nervous) it results to the touch: an appearance of higher consistency. c) defects superimposed to fruit (for instance sulphureous) and/or oxidised taste-aromas, in general: integrity vices worsen taste equilibrium, reinforcing the bitter taste.

THE METHOD TO MEASURE THE QUALITY OF WINE THROUGH TASTING

The overall evaluation of the quality – pleasantness – fruitiness is expressed assigning a mark in hundredths to tasted wine. Yet 100 is the non assignable score: the perfect wine that cannot be identified once and for all because there is and will always be the possibility of producing and tasting a wine better than the one ever produced or tasted so far. Therefore 99 is the highest assignable score: a wine presenting highest consistency, equilibrium and integrity, the wine incarnation of fruitiness, that is of pleasantness.

Such a score in ninety-ninths, equivalent to the Index of Pleasantness – quality of examined wine (IP), is obtained assigning a score from 1 to 33 to the consistency, the equilibrium, the integrity and then adding up the three assigned partial scores.

It is advisable the evaluation in tenths of each parameter level, converting mark in thirty-thirds according to equalities table of page 71 (Pic. 3).

VARIOUS INFORMATION ON THE INDEX OF PLEASANTNESS-QUALITY OF WINE

1) The higher is the quality of constituent fruit, the better the quality of wine obtained from this fruit. As regards to this, it must be considered that producers of best wines in the world are beforehand producers of the best grapes in the world.
2) The highest is the score in hundredths, the highest is the Index of Pleasantness – quality of evaluated wine.
3) Wines with equal overall pleasantness present different structure in taste as pointed out by dissimilar partials of consistency, equilibrium, and integrity.
4) In order to have an idea of the effective value of the score assigned in hundredths, it is necessary to put a comma between the first and the second figure of the evaluation. Thus a wine evaluated 67 points, in tenths is worth 6,7: in substance it is a wine tending from sufficient to good. A 70 point's wine is a wine worth 7,0: a good wine, even of unusual value. An 82 point's wine is a wine worth more than 8, a very good wine; and so on for wines around 90 points. A 92 point's wine is a wine worth 9,2, a wine truly excellent, very rare to be met and which is a great pleasure to be tasted. Percentage of recurrence (statistical value) of evaluations assigned during 1999 to the 5464 tasted wines is as follows. Below 60 points 0,04%; between 60 and 69 points 38,31%; between 70 and 79

points 57,92%; between 80 and 89 points 2,96%; between 90 and 99 points 0,77%; equal or more then 84 points (Wine-Fruit) 2,60%; equal or more than 78 points (wine worth Annuario dei Migliori Vini Italiani 2001) 5,87%.

5) Beginning from the level of quality – pleasantness – fruitiness expressed by the score 72 hundredths wines must be bought. Beginning from 84 hundredths the recall to constituent fruit is evident indeed; beginning from this threshold the quality – pleasantness – fruitiness of examined wine is really superior. Starting from this evaluation wines are Wine-Fruit, that is capable of recalling in a consistent, balanced and integral manner the constituent fruit. Wine-Fruit that will be marked by the following graphic sign:

CERTAINTY OF THE METHOD

- Being the three parameters determining wine pleasantness not only purely theoretical but also analytically measurable it is possible to verify objective truthfulness of sensorial evaluation released by the taster (analytical validation of assigned Index of Pleasantness – Quality).
- This method permits the evaluation of any kind of existing wine, realised everywhere, with any kind of grape, in any productive year (universality and absoluteness of evaluation).
- The isolated parameters are few but highly significant, in other words

they are macro-parameters: parameters implicating marginal but important different aspects in determination of wine quality (applicatory simplicity together with high significance).

- The isolated parameters are independent in commensuration (wide qualitative covering).
- The name and the meaning of the parameters are extra-slang, of universal and immediate comprehension (universal and direct communication, comprehension and usage).
- The overall pleasantness is the result of the sum of the three parameters determining it: it is the sum of consistency, equilibrium and integrity of taste (one is less reliable when directly evaluating overall pleasantness, because consideration of few aspects and of constituent detail might be omitted).
- Not only does this method permit the evaluation of the absolute pleasantness level of each wine, but it also explains how such an overall pleasantness is composed. Reading wine evaluation the reader knows the absolute value and can prefigure the constituent characteristics of the product (the pointing out of the intensity of the three parameters determining the score is the scattering of the absolute pleasantness).
- Between two wines of equal or analogous absolute pleasantness, this method allows the reader to buy the one which better meets with the characteristics more appreciated by the subject. The method permits to chose between two wines of analogous absolute value the more consistent, the more balanced, the more integral depending on the personal taste.
- This method makes producer know positive or negative sides of his wines to strengthen the ones or to correct the others, by means of a use-

ful and effective criticism. The scattering of pleasantness allows producers to address efficaciously their ameliorative efforts: indication and knowledge of the nature of the parameters andviticultural and oenological implications of each of them make it possible to producer the optimization of the intensity of every one of them.

Picture 3

Table of Conversion of decimal mark into score expressed in thirty-thirds

CONSISTENCY					EQUILIBRIUM					INTEGRITY				
Mark	10	=	33	Points	Mark	10	=	33	Points	Mark	10	=	33	Points
"	10 -	=	32	"	"	10 -	=	32	"	"	10 -	=	32	"
"	9 1/2	=	31	"	"	9 1/2	=	31	"	"	9 1/2	=	31	"
"	9	=	30	"	"	9	=	30	"	"	9	=	30	"
"	9 -	=	29	"	"	9 -	=	29	"	"	9 -	=	29	"
"	8 1/2	=	28	"	"	8 1/2	=	28	"	"	8 1/2	=	28	"
"	8	=	27	"	"	8	=	27	"	"	8	=	27	"
"	8 -	=	26	"	"	8 -	=	26	"	"	8 -	=	26	"
"	7 1/2	=	25	"	"	7 1/2	=	25	"	"	7 1/2	=	25	"
"	7	=	24	"	"	7	=	24	"	"	7	=	24	"
"	7 -	=	23	"	"	7 -	=	23	"	"	7 -	=	23	"
"	6 1/2	=	22	"	"	6 1/2	=	22	"	"	6 1/2	=	22	"
"	6 +	=	21	"	"	6 +	=	21	"	"	6 +	=	21	"
"	6	=	20	"	"	6	=	20	"	"	6	=	20	"
"	6 -	=	19	"	"	6 -	=	19	"	"	6 -	=	19	"
"	5 1/2	=	18	"	"	5 1/2	=	18	"	"	5 1/2	=	18	"
"	5	=	17	"	"	5	=	17	"	"	5	=	17	"
"	5 -	=	16	"	"	5 -	=	16	"	"	5 -	=	16	"
"	4 1/2	=	15	"	"	4 1/2	=	15	"	"	4 1/2	=	15	"
"	4 +	=	14	"	"	4 +	=	14	"	"	4 +	=	14	"

CHAPTER IV

INSIDE THE GLASS: PRACTICE

Practical application of the method: how to evaluate through tasting the index of Pleasantness-Quality of wine

The nucleus of tasting: to evaluate the intensity of the three parameters determining the Index of Pleasantness-Quality of wine

PRACTICAL APPLICATION OF THE METHOD: HOW TO EVALUATE THROUGH TASTING THE INDEX OF PLEASANTNESS-QUALITY OF WINE

In order to evaluate the Index of Pleasantness of a wine it is necessary to evaluate the intensity of the three parameters determining it: consistency, equilibrium, and integrity. Therefore while tasting it is necessary to wonder: which is the taste consistency, equilibrium and the taste integrity of this examined wine?

Giving a systematic answer to these questions the taster will receive from the glass the confirmation of the *Logisma* of the wine fruitiness and will learn the two laws by which it is regulated:

I) Only does a wine with a consistent, balanced and integral taste recall the constituent fruit (the grape).

II) The more a wine is capable of recalling the constituent fruit (the grape) in a consistent, balanced and integral way, the more pleasant it is.

Herebelow the rules and the basic principles for wine tasting

1) In order to precisely evaluate the intensity of each and everyone of the three parameters determining the pleasantness it is necessary to consider thoroughly the reflections of each of them (consistency, equilibrium and integrity) on: sight, smell and taste of examined wine.
2) In order to correctly apply the method it is necessary to evaluate one fundamental parameter after the other. First consistency, then equilibrium and after integrity. While evaluating consistency neither integrity nor equilibrium must be considered. Equilibrium can be estimated

just after consistency evaluation; integrity can be estimated after consistency and equilibrium evaluation: it is necessary to "vertically stay" on each parameter, without thinking to the parameter aside, or even weighing the other.

3) The very same value of a wine cannot qualify 2 fundamental parameters; the very same defect of a wine cannot penalise 2 fundamental parameters. If a wine is too bitter, its equilibrium and not its integrity must receive a low evaluation. On the single parameter it is necessary to stay vertically: don't consider integrity or consistency when equilibrium is analysed. The same should occur also for the evaluation of the other two parameters.
4) Consistency is esteemed mainly with the mouth, and thus equilibrium; on the other hand, integrity pertains to the nose.
5) A single aspect proposed by last tasted wine might help in attributing the correct evaluation to one of the three fundamental parameters of the wine tasted first. It is then possible to correct any mark assigned to every one of the tasted wines until tasting is definitively closed (a change of mind might be index of attention, that is of quality of application).
6) In order to precisely appraising the consistency it is necessary to have in mind the consistency of the best-tasted wine and to compare it to the one of the wine under examination; the same should be done for equilibrium and integrity.
7) In order to estimate consistency with precision it is useful to compare one another the consistency of tasted wines, the same should be done for equilibrium and taste integrity.
8) For tasting a wine in an accomplished manner, it is necessary to swal-

low at least a tiny sip of it. The first reason why this is necessary is to evaluate the equilibrium of taste after deglutition, thus isolating the intensity of the bitter sensation. The second is to check on uvula the integrity of wine. So we'd better distrust tasters who do not swallow.

Herebelow the test to perform in order to evaluate the Index of Pleasantness of a wine

The following is the succession of siftings that an examined wine should be subjected to (underlined sifting is the most significant and determinant for a true evaluation of the intensity of the referred parameter):

1) evaluation of visual consistency;
2) evaluation of olfactory consistency;
<u>3) evaluation of gustative consistency;</u>
4) mark from 1 to 33 to consistency;
5) evaluation of visual equilibrium;
6) evaluation of olfactory equilibrium;
<u>7) evaluation of gustative equilibrium;</u>
8) mark from 1 to 33 to equilibrium;
9) evaluation of visual integrity;
<u>10) evaluation of olfactory integrity;</u>
11) evaluation of gustative integrity;
12) mark from 1 to 33 to integrity;
13) addition of marks attributed to consistency, equilibrium, integrity = final centesimal mark = Index of Pleasantness – quality – fruitiness of tasted wine;
14) pondering and final check of the truthfulness of the evaluation. The

method was contrived so as to divert taster's attention from a direct evaluation of the overall pleasantness of tasted wine. If looking at a wine or just smelling it its overall quality index is at once estimated, it is not possible to mind the detail and its value is not analytically and methodically evaluated: thus issued judgement results less truthful and reliable. In fact if the index of quality is the result of the evaluation of the consistency, the equilibrium and the integrity and if the Index of Pleasantness is the overall sum of the qualifying aspects, esteem will carefully seize both whole value and constituent particular, thus giving a more reliable assessment because very detailed. It is anyway useful, after adding the three scores assigned to the three determining parameters, to consider the total score and evaluate its truthfulness in absolute terms. Therefore it is necessary to wonder "is examined wine really worth the obtained score?". It is very important to ask oneself and to reply to this question in order to critically weigh the validity of given estimation. If we think it's right then we'll pass to taste another wine, otherwise we'll go back and concentrate our perceptive attention once again on that examined wine in order to understand what we wrongly did during tasting and what to correct in our judgement. As regards to this it is useful to convert the evaluation from hundredths to tenths so as to take into consideration a figure easier to be evaluated: the majority of us has a greater confidence in perceiving the value of a product when expressed in tenths more then in hundredths. To achieve this is enough to put a comma or a point between the two figures of the centesimal evaluation. If after this we do not think the score is right in absolute terms and not adherent enough to the true merit of the examined wine, it is possible to correct the overall estimation modifying the evaluation given to one or more of the three fundamental parameters on the rise or on the fall (in conformity with rightness). Among the three parameters the one which seemed and we felt as less adhering to the true merit will be corrected: very useful a check to be performed in the case of a threshold assessment. If the sum of the three parameters is 69 points, that is 6,9 tenths, it is useful to wonder "is it a wine worth something less than 7 the one I am tasting, or is it a wine worth 7, that is 70? ". If the overall value of the examined wine will result as deserving a good mark – for example a full 7 – we can increase evaluation of the parameter consistency, if we have the feeling of being too severe in evaluating that aspect in the first instance. Or we'll modify the other two parameters in the same direction and measure, or with a different measure. The second thoughts are the symptom of the taster's attention. Notwithstanding my large experience, before evaluating in the most appropriate way the intensity of the parameters of certain wines I go back very often on the first evaluation. Thinking over is useful to perceive with the best possible precision the exact intensity of the evaluated parameter;

15) tale of perceived sensations, illustrating the superiority of examined wine with reference to each of the three fundamental parameters. Only after having estimated the intensity of the three parameters it is possible to narrate and describe the various sensations registered during the tasting. First the strict valuational aspect, that is the quantitative side, then the description of the nature of wine through the description of its principal merits, or through its more evident sensorial limits.

93 Luca Maroni • WINE TASTING exercise book

Wine name .... **Year** ....

Producer ....

Consistency		Equilibrium		Integrity		**Index of Pleasantness-Quality**
☐	+	☐	+	☐	=	☐

Sensations: ....

....

....

....

Date of tasting: ....

Wine name .... **Year** ....

Producer ....

Consistency		Equilibrium		Integrity		**Index of Pleasantness-Quality**
☐	+	☐	+	☐	=	☐

Sensations: ....

....

....

....

Date of tasting: ....

Picture 4

What observed to this point should be noted on a block notes, or on a schedule analogous to the one reproduced here above (compositional schedules of the exercise book "Wine Tasting": pic. 4).

THE NUCLEUS OF TASTING: TO EVALUATE THE INTENSITY OF THE THREE PARAMETERS DETERMINING THE INDEX OF PLEASANTNESS-QUALITY OF WINE

In order to evaluate the intensity of the three parameters determining the Index of Pleasantness of a wine, it is necessary to know the influence of the modification of each of them (consistency, equilibrium and integrity) on sight, smell and taste of examined wine. What does it change of the way wine results to the senses at the variation of the intensity of the three parameters during the three phases of tasting (visual, olfactory and gustative)? What is the effect on colour, on perfume and on taste of a high consistency, a low equilibrium and a good integrity? What do I have to observe or what do I have to feel to understand the true intensity level of each parameter? How do I have to act during the three phases of tasting to clearly perceive the intensity of the three parameters determining the Index of Pleasantness of a wine?
Hereafter the guiding lines to proceed in the most useful way to attain the purpose.

Evaluation of consistency

Wine consistency is estimated measuring the intensity of the colour, the quantity and the density of the perceived perfumes, and mainly the tactile sensation of the wine at the touch with the tongue.

The touch of wine is estimated introducing a small quantity of wine in the mouth and squeezing it between the tongue and the palate. Not much consistent a wine has a touch as fluid as water, very consistent a wine has a touch similar to the one – dense and viscous – of fruit juice.

Useful notes for a correct evaluation of consistency: a) differences in colour intensity between two white wines indicate diverse consistency levels only if wines are of the same year and were produced following analogous procedures. Oxidation (from wood or ageing) implies the increase of coloration of white wines that even if not rich in extract become intensely gilt as wines rich of body;

b) with equal consistency, the wine with more equilibrium will result denser and more viscous – softer – at the touch.

Reflections of changes of consistency on the three phases of tasting. At the variation of the consistency the way of each wine to result to senses change and wine behaviour during the three phases of tasting is different. So aspect, perfume and taste of a wine will be different being this wine more or less rich in consistency (more or less rich in extract). How is it possible then to measure with precision the intensity of the examined parameter, variable from wine to wine? Submitting tasted wine to visual, then olfactory and lastly gustative examination. During each examination it is necessary to attentively screen hereafter-described aspects (between brackets the percentage of significance level of each trial).

This is: a) what changes of any wine of its way to correlate with senses at variation of its consistency; b) what to evaluate of wine in the glass to understand with precision the level of its consistency in the sequence eye, nose and mouth.

Consistency and eye (significant at 10%):

1) *Quantity-intensity of coloration:* a wine rich in extractive substances is for this reason rich in colouring substances. The more a wine is consistent, the more it is coloured;

2) *visual viscosity of the liquid, small arches on the surface of the glass:* with reference to this, let us ponder this series of synonymous: consistency = concentration = density = viscosity = friction = hindering to movement. Conferring a glass a rotating movement equal to 1, if wine contained is not much consistent it will not meet friction rotating on the glass side and therefore it will move equally to given thrust. In fact, if wine is concentrated and dense, with a thrust equal to 1 friction and hindering to movement of such a rich liquid will restrain rotation and wine will move up to 0,8 (in substance it will absorb part of the thrust itself). A wine rich in extracts is restive at moving inside the glass, it will move "fat", designing on the inner face of the goblet arcades restive at detaching from crystal, slow at rejoining the wine disk when glass stands still.

Consistency and nose (significant at 20%):

1) *Quantity-intensity of perfumes:* it is obvious that a fruit compote put on a plate smells more than one single fruit put on the same plate. A wine rich in extractive substances is for this reason rich in aromatic substances: the more a wine is consistent, the more intense is its perfume.

2) *Olfactory density of the liquid (clothing grade of olfaction):* the nose is perfectly capable of perceiving the density, therefore the extractive concentration of the smelt solution. If, with blindfolded eyes, you smell two glasses full of an odourless but differently consistent solution - for instance water and milk - this is immediately recognised thanks to its denser, thicker,

gummier smell. In accordance with this phenomenon the more wine is consistent, the more its smell is dense, thick and often sort of soft. The olfaction, the portion of air inhaled by the nostrils, when coming from a diluted wine proposes a smell of contact with wine itself (generally acid-alcoholic), then it does not register smells any more and goes on as naked, only airy. Vice versa, the olfaction of consistent wines feels dense the contact odour and therefore the entire remaining inhalatory stream is dressed of fruit perfume: odourless air is no more felt. Also the conclusive part of olfaction is dressed with aromas, seen abundance of aromatic substances in the solution. Although the taster deeply and long inhales he always smells perfume, never air devoid of any odour (see Pic. 5).

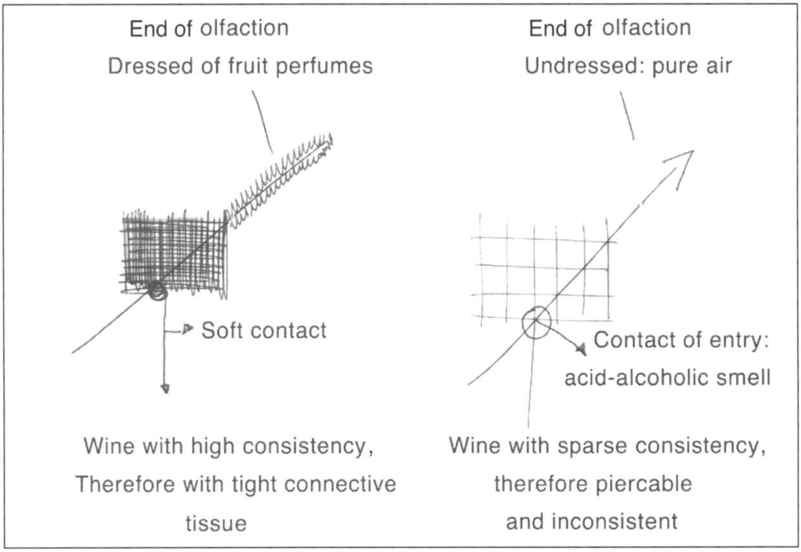

Picture 5

Consistency and mouth (significant at 70%):

1) *touch of wine (watery or viscous):* water, containing extracts between 0,1 and 0,5 g/l and in substance devoid of consistency, results at the touch extremely fluid, diluted per definition at maximum grade. Milk - thicker - has an average of extracts between 15 and 17 g/l. Wine, from 16 g/l of extract of less consistent white wines, arrives to 40 g/l of richest red wines. Fruit juice owes its marvellous density and creaminess to its superior richness: extracts between 70 and 80 g/l. There, between 16 and 40 g/l of extracts, all the increasing viscosities of contact of wine are included. If wine touches as watery as water, has a low extractive consistency. If wine touches dense and creamy, if contact thanks to its viscosity is similar to the one of fruit juice, it has a high consistency. Use the mouth as a scale and feel the touch of wine, thanks to the perceptive sensitivity of our buccal cavity that feels a hair in the mouth as a trunk in a stream (hair diameter = 0, 3 microns of millimetre).

2) *Quantity-intensity-persistency of the flavour after deglutition:* the more consistent is a wine, the stronger is the click of its taste when swallowed, the longer is the persistency of its flavour in the mouth.

Table of picture n. 6 schematises the variations of the sensorial characteristics of white and red wines at the modification of consistency. It is a useful summarising prospect for a correct evaluation of the parameter.

White wines			
CONSISTENCY	Low	Medium	High
Visual examination:	Neutral colour, whitish, very fluent a liquid at rotating movement of the glass	Yellow colour appears, midway fluent a liquid at rotating movement of the glass	Strong yellow, golden, viscous a liquid at rotating movement of the glass
Olfactory examination:	Not much perfumes, neutral smell with notes of yeast in excess, olfactory sensations devoid of intensity	Moderate quantity of perfumes, olfactory sensations of a certain intensity	Abundant and dense perfumes
Gustative examination:	Not much taste, diluted touch, fluent, watery	Good quantity of taste, midway dense and viscous a touch	Abundant taste, dense and viscous touch, long persistency
Suggested marks:	from 1 to 20	from 21 to 25	from 26 to 33

Red wines			
CONSISTENCY	Low	Medium	High
Visual examination:	Ruby red colour, diffusely transparent, very fluent at rotating movement of the glass	Intense red midway transparent, midway fluent at rotating movement of the glass	Opaque red, viscous at rotating movement of the glass
Olfactory examination:	Not much perfumes, neutral smell with notes of yeast in excess, olfactory sensations devoid of intensity	Moderate quantity of perfumes, olfactory sensations of a certain intensity	Abundant and dense perfumes .
Gustative examination:	Not much taste, diluted touch, fluent, watery	Good quantity of taste, midway dense and viscous a touch	Abundant taste, dense and viscous touch, long persistency
Suggested marks:	from 1 to 20	from 21 to 25	from 26 to 33

Picture 6

Evaluation of Equilibrium

The equilibrium of wine is evaluated tasting a small quantity of it and evaluating the harmony or the disequilibrium of the taste, that is evaluating the superiority of the tasted wine with reference to the fundamental equation of the gustative equilibrium:

Eq = Sweet Taste Substances =

Acid Taste Substances + Bitter Taste Substances

Wine equilibrium is evaluated analysing the shades of the hue, the quality and the "shape" of the perceived perfumes, mainly the balance between soft and acid-bitter sensations of taste. A not much balanced wine has sharpened and acid-bitter smells, acid or acid-bitter taste.

Useful notes for a correct evaluation of the equilibrium: a) in comparison to the not-balanced, balanced wine seems not to have perfumes, in reality it does not have sharp or defective peaks (mistrust what stands out because in the wine field taste disequilibrium and/or defect do). b) a white wine not balanced because immature may present warm and golden tones of colour due to oxidation; this is why visual examination is not very significant for white wines.

Reflections of changes of the equilibrium on the three phases of the tasting. At variation of the equilibrium the way of each wine to result to senses change and wine behaviour during the three phases of tasting is different. So aspect, perfume and taste of a wine will be different being this wine more or less balanced. How is it possible then to measure with precision the intensity of the examined parameter, variable from wine to wine? Submitting tasted wine to visual, then olfactory and lastly gustative examination. During each examination it is necessary to attentively screen hereafter-described aspects (between brackets percentage of significance level of each trial).

This is a) what changes of any wine of its way to correlate with senses at the variation of its equilibrium; b) what to evaluate of the wine in the glass to understand with precision the level of its equilibrium in the sequence eye, nose and mouth.

Equilibrium and eye (significant at 10%):

1) *shades and tints of coloration:* a not balanced since immature white wine has grey-green tints and a cold hue. With increase of wine pH, and related ripeness increase of used constituent fruit, the colour gets warmer and yel-

low colour appears; a balanced white wine with high pH has golden yellow tints (a chromatic progression identical to the natural one of white grape). A sour red wine has bright ruby red tints; at pH increase colour gets warmer and becomes darker to burgundy; a balanced red with high pH has purple-blackish tints (a chromatic progression identical to the natural one of red grape). The examination of the nuances is the more significant, the less a wine is oxidised (oxidation modifies the tints of hue).

Equilibrium and nose (significant at 25%):

1) *geometrical shape of the smells:* let's smell a wine and feel if its smell is sharp or round: both peaks deriving to wine from the deficiency of equilibrium in the components. Excesses of bitterness and acidity make olfaction spiked, pointed and aggressive. In fact smells of a balanced wine have a round and encircling shape. The perfume disposition, beginning from unbreathable volatile acidity (thus because so sharpen to be acetously and vertically rectilinear), arrives to horizontal grapy roundness of balanced wines. Hence a smell disposition from vertical to horizontal: from repelling to inviting, from concave to convex smells (see Pic. 7);

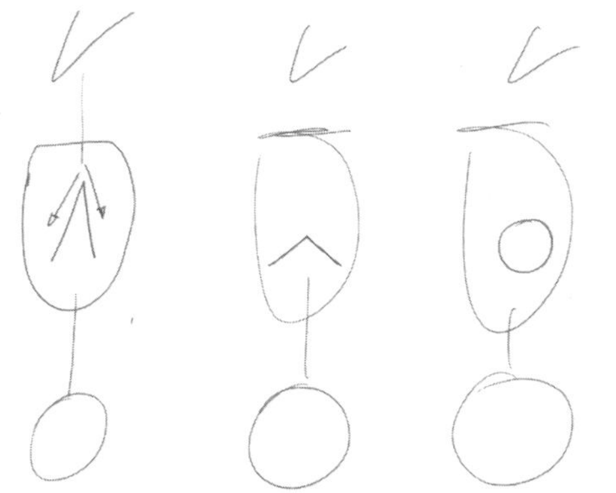

Picture 7

2) *dominating olfactory trend:* an acid wine has an acid odour, a bitter wine has a bitter smell: examples of disequilibrium which render a perfume not soft and suasive. An immature wine has a sour scent, a bitter one has medicinal and leather-like smell: a midway balanced wine has a fragrance in which the softness appears, a balanced one has a sweetly and suasively grapy smell. Balanced wines have a scent in which grape, or other ripe fruits, are very evident: a balanced wine gives the nose fruit notes;

3) *analogical olfactory recalls:* white wines not in equilibrium for acidity excess have smells recalling lemons, grape-fruit, magnesia; bitterness in white wines gives notes of almonds. Unbalanced red wines recall liquorice: analogy produced by the convergence of the tannin on lemony base (lemon + tannin = liquorice). Balanced wines recall grape or not citrus fruits, ripe and sweet ones.

Equilibrium and mouth (significant at 65%):

1) *evaluation of the taste of wine:* let's taste wine, appreciate its taste evaluating the harmony or the disequilibrium of its taste, in other words the balance between sweet sensations and the sum of the acid and the bitter ones. Let's evaluate in substance if the taste of wine is as soft as acid bitter. After all evaluate the superiority of its taste with reference to the equation of the gustative equilibrium (Eq = Sweet Taste Substances = Acid Taste Substances + Bitter Taste Substances). While tasting it is fundamental to put oneself in the place of non-keen and non-regular consumers: so do not keep wine in the mouth for long time, sweetening it with the softening saliva. Let's put wine in our mouth and let's directly swallow it to feel its taste; let's drink wine as all the others do, like water and/or any other drink. After evaluating with a small sip overall equilibrium of the taste, we can submit the taste of the wine we are drinking to a more technical screen in order to understand if the disequilibrium perceived was caused by an excess of acidity or bitterness. Acidity is evaluated while wine is in the mouth, before deglutition, opening mouth a little and evaluating more or less sourness on the sides of the tongue. Bitterness is evaluated in the moment of the deglutition, when wine passes in oesophagus, and after it is swallowed. In other words the bitter is felt when wine is no more in the mouth. Bitter wine has a bitter taste end far less balanced than the taste in the mouth. Bitter wines close in the stomach and this is why they are penetrating and heavy and leave an unpleasant taste of smoke and chinaroot in the mouth. The check of post-deglutition taste equilibrium, useful to isolate intensity of bitter sensation, is the first reason why it is necessary to swallow wine in order to taste it in the most accomplished manner. This in another reason to mistrust tasters who do not swallow.

White wines			
EQUILIBRIUM	Low	Medium	High
Visual examination:	Cold nuances of basic light yellow: grey-green	Yellow shades	Golden yellow shades
Olfactory examination:	Intense, vibrating perfumes, with analogies with lemons or grapefruit. The shape of the smells is pointed, acute	Perfumes of good wideness, between acid and soft. The shape of the smells is less pointed and acute	Perfumes basically soft, sweet, arranged in wideness. The shape of the smells is round and encircling
Gustative examination:	Excess of the acid and/or bitter sensations on the soft ones: hard taste	Light excess of the acid-bitter sensations on soft ones: taste almost balanced	Balanced, pleasant, soft, complex taste
Suggested marks:	from 1 to 20	from 21 to 25	from 26 to 33

Red wines			
EQUILIBRIUM	Low	Medium	High
Visual examination:	Bright nuances – ruby colour – of basic red	Cherry red-burgundy shades of basic red	Egg plant peel and blackish nuances of basic red
Olfactory examination:	Intense, sour and/or bitter perfumes, analogies with liquorice, lemon, rhubarb (over tannic wines)	Perfumes of good wideness, between acid and soft. The shape of the smells is less pointed and acute	Perfumes basically soft, sweet, arranged in wideness. The shape of the smells is round and encircling
Gustative examination:	Excess of acid and/or bitter sensations on the soft ones: not much pleasant taste	Light excess of the acid-bitter sensations on the soft ones: taste almost balanced	Balanced, pleasant, soft complex taste
Suggested marks:	from 1 to 20	from 21 to 25	from 26 to 33

Picture 8

Table of picture n. 8 schematises the variations of the sensorial characteristics of white and red wines at the modification of the equilibrium. It is a useful summarising prospect for a correct evaluation of the parameter.

Evaluation of Integrity

Integrity is evaluated analysing the visual aspect, the limpidness and the freshness of the perceived taste-aromas. Not much integral a wine has defective and old smells, taste not much clean and oxidised. A wine with low integrity does not recall the fruit it is made of. Integral a wine doesn't have any cleanliness defect, it is not oxidised and this is why it recalls the constituent fruit: the grape.

Useful notes for a correct evaluation of integrity: a) very seldom a wine presents just one isolated defect of integrity: often a wine is affected by several vices at the same time (the integrity is a parameter depending on operator's diligence: if he is not diligent not one but one thousand defects arise). b) let's imagine integrity as a bar more or less present, transparent and distorting between the taster and the consistency and the equilibrium of a wine: C E| I (non integral a wine); C E¦I (wine midway integral); C E I (integral wine).

Reflections of the changes of the integrity on the three phases of the tasting. At variation of the integrity the way of each wine to result to senses changes and wine behaviour during the three phases of tasting is different. So the aspect, the perfume and the taste of a wine will be different being this wine more or less integral. How is it possible then to measure with precision the intensity of the examined parameter, variable from wine to wine? Submitting tasted wine to visual, then olfactory and lastly gustative examination. During each examination it is necessary to attentively screen hereafter-described aspects (between brackets the percentage of significance level of each trial). This is a) what changes of any wine of its way to correlate with senses at the variation of its integrity; b) what to evaluate of the wine in the glass to understand with precision the level of its integrity in the sequence eye, nose and mouth.

Integrity and eye (significant at 10%):

1) *shades and tints of coloration:* the 5 possible cleanliness defects (sulphur, ace-

tous, woody, milky and vanished) do not have optical relevance: the visual examination is therefore not significant to estimate the cleanliness level of a wine, but it is very significant for the evaluation of the newness of a wine (oxidation grade). The most important reverberation of the oxidation is exactly the progressive change of the hue tints. A new white wine has a colour whose chromatic charge is entirely imputable to its consistency, in other words to its richness in extracts. With time passing the colour overburdens due to the yellowing and darkening of the oxidable substances (polyphones). In white wines, tints from bright yellow become brown, nut colour, mahogany. In red wines the oxidation increase inflames yellow shades, beforehand visible only where the wine thickness diminished (on the crystal edge), then in all the zones of the glass with colour change from blackish burgundy to garnet red, brick brown and brick orange.

Integrity and nose (significant at 70%):

1) *integrity of smells:* fruitiness level of perfumes: presence of clean and fresh perfumes of grape or other natural fruits. Nose is a fantastic receiver of integrity and vice versa of stinks, deviations, anomalies and degradations. If a wine has cleanliness vices or if it has oxidised aromas, its perfume does not recall grape or any other fruit. Let's put our nose on wine and let's wonder: is there fruit? If yes, wine is integral. If no, wine is not integral. Hence let's evaluate from 1 to 10 the level of fruitiness, in other words the level of cleanliness and newness of the smell we perceive. The technicians will have to go forward and to identify the reason of the fruit absence from the perfumes, in other words they will have to figure out the nature of the contaminating agent and/or the level of the perfume degradation. In this case it will be useful to proceed by elimination, evaluating

in complete sequence the presence of one or more perfume defects: unclean smell is sulphureous, is it acetous, is it ligneous, is it milky, vanished? Is there any note of rancid or of almond in the perfume of this white, or is there any caramel and Madeira notes in the one of this red? With the growing of the experience it will no longer be necessary to wonder if we distinguish or we don't each one of the defects: the defect or the defects will be analytically recognised at the examination of the registered perfume.

Integrity and mouth (significant at 20%):

1) *cleanliness and freshness of taste:* clean and fresh a taste, not spicy, non acetous, non woody or milky or vanished, rancid, sugary or old;

2) *wine behaviour on uvula, during deglutition:* while swallowing wine is obliged to touch uvula, passing through a rectilinear corridor (see Pic. 9). Uvula is not situated in the centre of the throat by chance: it is a perfect integrity catcher. Integral wine is not felt on uvula: its transit does not modify uvula's state of rest. Vice versa the unclean wine (faulty and defective) differently sensitises the uvula. When swallowed a sulphureous wine scrapes and pinches the uvula in a spicy way; an acetous wine vibrates, stings and pseudo-thermally sensitises the uvula (there it might reveal itself as cold-hot); a woody wine bittery dulls the uvula; a milky one is less vibrating then the acetous one; the vanished also is lightly vibrating. The control of wine integrity at uvula touch is the second reason why it is necessary to swallow wine in order to taste it in the most accomplished manner (the first is the control of the intensity of the bitterness sensation while evaluating the equilibrium). Mistrust also for this reason the tasters who do not swallow.

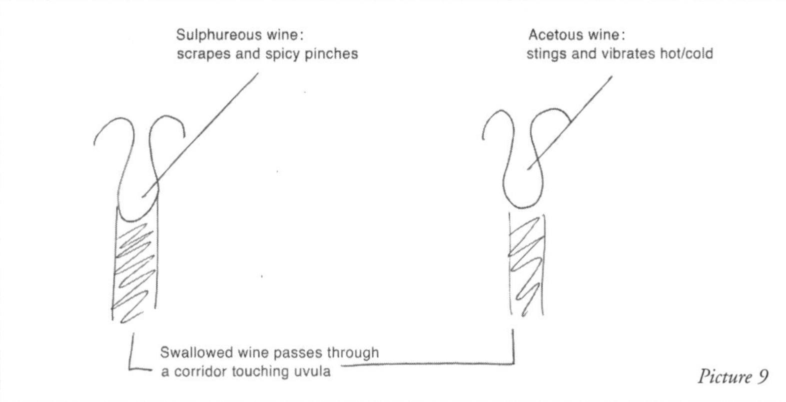

Picture 9

White wines			
INTEGRITY	Low	Medium	High
Visual examination	Brown shades of basic yellow hue	Golden shades of basic yellow hue	Bright shades of basic yellow hue
Olfactory examination:	Not much clean perfumes (sulphureous, milky, woody acetous, etc) and/or more or less toasted and rancid	Midway clean and fresh perfumes	Clean and very fresh perfumes, clear recall to grape or other fruits
Gustative examination:	Not much clean tastes (sulphureous, milky, woody acetous, etc) and/or more or less toasted and rancid	Midway clean and fresh tastes	Clean and very fresh tastes
Suggested marks:	from 1 to 20	from 21 to 25	from 26 to 33

Red wines			
INTEGRITY	Low	Medium	High
Visual examination	Orange juice hue and brick tints of basic red	Lightly orange shades (on wine edge) of basic red	Strong and lively purple shades of basic red
Olfactory examination:	Not much clean perfumes (sulphureous, milky, woody acetous, etc) and/or more or less toasted and rancid	Midway clean and fresh perfumes	Clean and very fresh perfumes, clear recall to grape or other fruits
Gustative examination:	Not much clean tastes (sulphureous, milky, woody, acetous, etc.) and/or more or less rancid and caramel like, bitter-sweetish	Midway clean and fresh tastes	Clean and very fresh tastes
Suggested marks:	from 1 to 20	from 21 to 25	from 26 to 33

Picture 10

The table of picture n. 10 schematises the variations of the sensorial characteristics of white and red wines at the modification of the integrity. It is a useful summarising prospect for a correct evaluation of the parameter.

CHAPTER V

THE INDEX OF PLEASANTNESS OF WINE THROUGH TIME

EFFECTS OF TIME PASSING ON THE THREE PARAMETERS DETERMINING THE QUALITY OF WINE

The producer himself with conclusive bottling definitively fixes the Index of Pleasantness of examined wine. With the bottling the analytical merits of the three parameters determining wine quality are fixed.

Knowing the analytical nature of these parameters we can see what objectively occurs to each one of them with time passing and with wine staying in the bottle.

Consistency, that is wine richness in extracts, is analytically stable with a trend to slight decrease (-3/6% in ten years). With time passing and under the point of view of the extracts white wines can either remain unaltered or can give rise to small tartaric precipitations: those crystalline deposits that only very rich in extracts white wines present when mature. Red wines may give rise to more relevant a deposit: in fact they are differently rich in polyphenols and tannins that with time aggregate in compounds with too heavy a molecular weight to remain in solution. Therefore the deposits should not be considered as any defect sign but as the sign of ripeness and extractive richness of that wine showing them. But never with time passing shall we find a wine more consistent than it was when young. The extract is not auto-generated thanks to time passing.

Wine equilibrium, that is the harmonic taste balance piloted by pH among diverse wine constituents, is analytically stable with trend to decrease. It is so important that wine pH does not change with time, that nature provides pH with a buffer, with a protection of variable strength in order to keep wine pH fix and unaltered (higher or lower buffer power). In fact, under a sensorial point of view the equilibrium of the taste tends to decrease. With the progressive increase of oxidised substances (disaggregated and made decrepit by time passing) the intensity of acid and bitter sensations augments, with stable or minor intensity of the sensation of sweet. The oxidised substances have a rancid taste, that is acid-bitter, not soft and this does not occur for wine only. From what said so far: 1) if a wine enters a bottle as balanced, it remains like this progressively less with time passing; 2) if a wine enters the bottle as unbalanced because more acid-bitter than soft, with ageing it becomes more and more unbalanced. Only when the level of extractive substance decay is nearly complete and only when at last pH moves from its original value, wine, now completely and irreversibly Madeirised, results sweet and slightly sweet sour, unpleasantly mellifluous at taste.

Wine integrity progressively decreases with time. As far as the cleanliness is concerned if a wine is sulphureous, acetous, woody, vanished or milky the presence of one or more amongst these defects is absolutely insensible to time passing. If a wine enters the bottle as faulty, it will always be forever. Just as the consistency is not auto-generated in the bottle with time passing, in the very same way a defect cannot pass or arise. As far as the newness is concerned, or in fact as oxidation, this progressively increases as time goes by.

From what said to this point, it results the tendential and progressive analytical reduction of the index of quality of wines. Hence given the original level of consistency, equilibrium and integrity the time passing determines a gradual decrease of the Index of Pleasantness of any existing wine.

WINE DOES NOT IMPROVE WITH TIME

As it occurs to every one of us approaching wine I derived from the classical texts the notion that wine improves with time. And at the first moment, with the natural good faith of someone coming closer to something he doesn't directly knows, I really trusted such an assumption. Facing a not much pleasant wine, just as some producers and tasters yet use to say, I said to myself "this wine is not ready, today it is not pleasant but in a few years it will be fantastic". But getting more and more acquainted and becoming from lover a professional taster, I decided to scientifically verify the validity of this commonplace, one of the most diffused and uncritically shared by the people relating to wine. I decided to investigate with method. So I established a new branch of tasting: the organoleptical – dynamic analysis. I used to buy a certain wine in 12 samples, tasting a new bottle every six months/one-year after former tasting. On a page of my technical magazine, in a survey called "Observatory: organoleptical – dynamic analysis" in order to verify and isolate the effects of ageing, I used to publish the descriptive schedules of the same wine comparing between themselves different profiles subsequently noticed. Instead of perceiving a certain improvement of wine, in other words an increase of its consistency, equilibrium or integrity, inevitably I used to find the wine or inexorably identical to itself, or progressively less balanced and mainly less integral. I submitted to this observatory more than one hundred wines of diverse origins and years, produced everywhere from whichever kind of grape. After seven years of such an exercise, after noticing every time what is observed and described in the former paragraph, I cancelled the survey. As it must be, time passing in 100% of the

observed cases gave as a result a progressive, slow decrease of the organoleptical characteristics of all the examined wines.
The myth of an always-improving wine is perhaps the brightest pearl of an abstruse and untrue way of illustrating and perceiving wine. A conception extremely detrimental for wine, of course encouraged by the producers who have the highest interest in seeing their wines evaluated not in a negative way ("if a certain wine is not pleasant at the moment in which it is commercialised, it is not producer's responsibility. Fault belongs to people who taste wine too early, when it is not yet ready - ?!? –").
So the false myth of a wine improved by time passing adopted, enhanced and uncritically accepted by specialised "critic", in fact allowed several producers to put on the market wines with non-optimal initial consistency, equilibrium and integrity. And what is even worst is that the producers and the "experts" have defined these wines as wines that will be very good after the ageing. Exactly the opposite of the true because with time the defects do not disappear but increase and the merits progressively decrease. Nurturing this myth really damaged the wine field that instead of concentrating resources on the effective technical improvement of the product, preferred to take economical advantage of the good faith of other people's giving out the evident actual defects as potential and future merits. If today wine is not yet systematically pleasant as main part of edible aliments are at the moment of their introduction into the market, this is uniquely due to the false myth of wine improving with time. In fact it is not perceived as fundamental to produce an immediately pleasant wine if pleasantness itself is anyway achieved through simple time passing. For what observed so far, the real wine lover must be intransigent on this point: from the very beginning the wine must be the more consistent, bal-

anced and integral possible as the passing of time will imply the substantial seal and the gradual diminution of the intensity of the three parameters determining its quality. Said all this about the non-truthfulness of the assumption; it is worth wondering on how and why the idea "wine improves with time passing" gained ground. Given the technical and the technological scarcity of oenology in the past, until 1955 all wines were strongly acetous. The only system to drink with a kind of a pleasure a wine thus acetous was that of letting it oxidise in such an evident and pronounced way that the mellifluous extra-sweet Madeirisation could balance the sharp acetous otherwise too harsh and penetrating to be inhaled and swallowed (acetous x Madeira = fruit – like). But today when the wines are born integral, round and soft, now that the acetous straight line is neutralised, there is no reason to age them for long. In fact wines should be produced with a newness as intact as possible because the best way to render a wine capable of remaining pleasant for a long period in the bottle is that of keeping the most integral possible the original freshness of the fruit from which it was created.

WINE LASTS THROUGH TIME

This is the real plus of the wine. It is not its non-existing capacity of meliorating with time passing, but its substantial capacity of lasting for a long time and being pleasant through time. It is the positive effect of alcohol, the characterising element of wine, which acts as time delayer of the processes of degradation. This is how, thanks to alcohol, the taste-aromatic contents of beverage-wine instead of degrading quite quickly, loses with progressive slowness its sensorial virtues thus wine resulting drinkable for a very wide temporal arch. Alcohol acts as a protective screen of constituent wine elements, assuring their survival at an appreciable level of integrity for a period of time much longer than the one necessary to other aliments to become decrepit. As a matter of fact wine is the only pleasantly usable sensorial archive of the agricultural production worldwide. If I want to taste an earth product for instance dated 1990, I can only drink a bottle of wine. And this is the miracle. This is the principle at the basis of the increase of wine value through time. Today there are very many bottles on the market of recent years, very few, rare and therefore of a great and increasing value the items of older years still enjoyable in a pleasant manner. Fair enough, with time the economical evaluation of wine is revalued: for any passing year the existence in life of a certain vintage, and especially if it is a good one, is a fact always more rare and therefore more precious.

POTENTIAL LONGEVITY

Wine capacity of lasting through time relies on two factors: on its consistency and on oxidative integrity with which that wine reaches the bottle. The more consistent and less oxidised the wine is at the moment of bottling, the longer its potential residual arch of life is. This is why it is detrimental to age wine for too long a period. A wine starting yet oxidised, dark if white, orange if red is less long-lived of another identically rich in extracts but not oxidised. The wines aged for long cannot be at the same time wines worth long ageing. Only by keeping intact the original freshness of the fruit the potential longevity of a wine is maximised. The less a wine is oxidised at the moment of bottling, the longer it will live getting oxidised the later. Under a merely extractive point of view, white wines with consistency evaluated between 20 and 24 points result pleasantly drinkable during the year, year and a half after vintage indication on label. Between 25 and 28 points in the two, three subsequent years; over 28 points in the four and more subsequent years. For the red wines, wines with consistency between 24 and 26 points result pleasantly drinkable during the two-three years and a half after vintage indication. Between 27 and 28 points in the three-five subsequent years; between 29 and 30 points in the five-seven subsequent years; over 30 points in the ten and more years after vintage. Under a general point of view, so that the reported values are actual indicators of residual potential longevity, it is necessary that the oxidation level of diverse wines is absolutely optimised – tending to zero – at the moment of entering the market.

THE PROGRESSIVE ACTION OF THE OXIDATION

The oxidation gradually acts day after day rendering less sprightly and fresh the profile wine had when bottled.

To the wine it occurs what happens to a newspaper abandoned on the dashboard of our car. The first day it is white, absolutely integral. The second day a kind of a film, a yellowish patina will begin to form on it, progressively increasing of intensity. The third day it is a little more yellow, after a month it is dark, after a year it will tend to brown. But just as the increase of the oxidised patina renders it more difficult the perceivement of the picture reported on the first page of the newspaper (without modifying under any extent the essential nature of that picture: a circle does not become a square or vice versa), thus any kind of wine after a certain

period of time will be consistent and balanced in the same way but less integral, that is less sound, less fresh, if we want more veiled.
Let's graphically represent wine-fruit and compare its oxidative dynamic with a wine with exactly opposing characteristics. The consistency, in other words the constituent plot or the intimate connective tissue of a wine, is represented on pic. 11 with the density of stroke; the equilibrium with the roundness, the integrity with the perfect definition and the closing of the circle (wine n. 1). The wine with a low Index of Pleasantness is not much consistent and has an extractive plot - and hence graphic stroke - large (a kind of fisherman's net). If it is not much balanced it has sharp smell and taste in fact the figure is not perfectly closed because threadbare, corroded, outlined by oxidation (wine n. 2). This the state of wines at the moment of bottling. After the first year of ageing the film begins to form; after two years the film is more intense, after three years even more and so on. On the one hand the wine with low index of quality (not much consistent, balanced and integral) immediately after the first year is perceived as much less pleasant due to oxidation, on the other wine-fruit immediately pleasant is a little bit less pleasant through time. On the contrary, the qualitative differences between a wine with low index of quality and a wine with a high index tend with time passing to become more and more evident. After all and once again the more a wine is qualitative (consistent, balanced and integral) when young, the more it will be when old.

TASTE-FLAVOUR COMBINATIONS OF THE EVOLUTION

It is always necessary to keep in mind that any perfume or taste we perceive when tasting a wine of any age is the sensorial result of its chemical

Picture 11

constituent components. Bringing the nose near to a glass I perceive a block, an ensemble of sensations both positive and negative. In a wine the more active are qualitative chemical components, the more this wine will result pleasant at tasting. Then let's say that the perfume of wine *X* that we perceive on a certain moment is equal to 100. So we are supposing that at the moment of bottling examined wine is absolutely perfect as far as oxidative integrity is concerned. We can begin following this wine through time.

At the beginning we have said that the overall perfume, worth 100 points at the start, is entirely due to the sensorial reflection of the present Alive Taste Substances (ATS). After two years I will perceive the same perfume worth 100 but this will not be constituted by ATS only, 70 ATS and 30 Oxidised Taste Substances (OTS) will form it. Five years later overall registered perfume could be due to 55 ATS and 45 OTS, after ten years we can have 30 residual ATS and 70 increasing OTS.

The preference recognised by everyone to the sensorial shades due to the oxidation, to the ideal mix between ATS and OTS (visualised and described on Picture 12), therefore the decision referred to the optimal moment for consumption of a certain wine is a subjective and cultural matter. Subjective because certain people prefer wines sensations of which are absolutely fresh and perfectly integral, some others prefer wines with diverse combinations between ATS and OTS and some other people love wines decidedly oxidised. Cultural because people who love evolved wines belong to less recent generations sensorially formed in a period in which it was technically difficult to prevent and control the oxidation. These people have senses used to feel as congenital and ingrained the lack of freshness in wine. This while youngsters, culturally used and grown up drinking beverages with an integrity absolutely perfect often do not drink wine because they find it unpleasantly old at taste.

Whichever your personal preference could be, only a wine perfectly integral at the moment of the introduction into the market is capable of satisfying with the evolution everybody's taste. In fact while a wine with perfect initial oxidative integrity (and therefore preferred by young people) with time acquires those oxidised nuances dear to the historical wine consumers, it is not true the opposite. A wine that is born oxidised is already targeted to a smaller public also destined to die out. And this without taking into consideration the fact that a wine that is born even only partially oxidised is a wine which is less worth investing on because lacking in oxidative integrity and therefore not very long-lived. Logical: the less a wine is oxidised at the start, the more it is potentially long-lived (the greater the shelf-life of the product), the higher its analytical and commercial value.

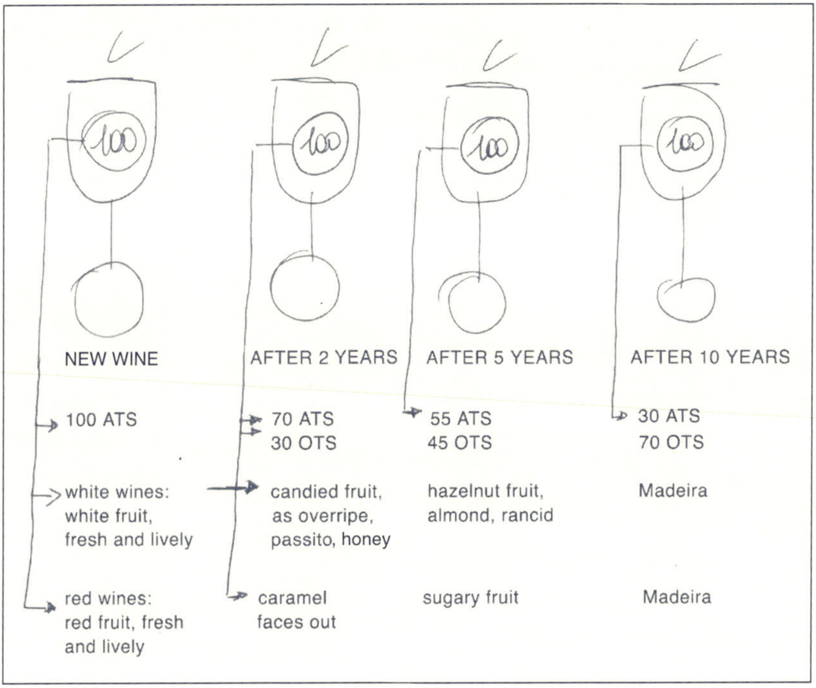
100
100
100
100
NEW WINE
AFTER 2 YEARS
AFTER 5 YEARS
AFTER 10 YEARS
100 ATS
70 ATS
30 OTS
55 ATS
45 OTS
30 ATS
70 OTS
white wines:
white fruit,
fresh and lively
candied fruit,
as overripe,
passito, honey
hazelnut fruit,
almond, rancid
Madeira
red wines:
red fruit, fresh
and lively
caramel
faces out
sugary fruit
Madeira

Picture 12

CHAPTER VI

FOOD-WINE MARRIAGES

THE BEST MARRIAGE

Before going into the detail of the technique of linkages it is opportune to observe what follows. Food is not eaten in the same moment in which wine is drunk. Almost never they are together in the mouth. Hence the lingual receptors do not evaluate the taste of a liquid-solid swill. First, food is eaten and its aroma and taste are fully appreciated. Afterwards, having in the mouth only the aromatic stream of the swallowed morsel, wine is tasted and its own aromatic stream will be perceived. So it is important: 1) to avoid screeches between these two taste givers and their taste streams; 2) maximise both the pleasures.

If the main objective is to maximise the pleasure obtainable in sequence by the courses and the drinks foreseen during a meal, then the best linkage is that between the preferred wine and the preferred dish. In other words trying to taste as many morsels of the favourite dish followed by diverse sips of the favourite wine.

One thing is absolutely certain: a mediocre course does not become good thanks to its marriage with an excellent wine and vice versa. Just as any course, any wine must be good in itself, and if it needs a dish to become good, for instance to balance its acidity, it means that that wine in itself is not worth much.

Besides, it is just ridiculous the idea that good wines should only be tasted with high cuisine dishes. That's enough with the story of the red wines reserved to noble poultry, hunting and game.

Up with the red wines (and the whites) that you love together with the dishes you prefer most.

Another concept very important to be considered: changing the wine during a meal does not generate any headache or drunkenness. This would occur if you drink too much, and not if only a moderate quantity of different wines is drunk. It is the absolute quantity of drunk wine that must be controlled: you do not have to exceed a given overall threshold of wine but the quality of diverse wines that sum up to that threshold is not determining. Of course the change of the taste between one wine and another provokes the desire to taste new sips but it does not generate any kind of physiological - digestive problems. After all the quantitative moderation permits the qualitative variability. In wine-food marriages the personal taste is the main objective to be fulfilled. This also considering that there exist some gustative interactions between liquid and food capable of amplifying, increasing and proposing a resulting taste even more pleasant than the two prime ones.

RULES FOR FOOD-WINE MARRIAGES

The first main rule: to harmonise the consistency and the equilibrium of the tastes. We'll move considering the parameters consistency and equilibrium of the course and the wines to be linked.
Consistency: a dish with a consistent taste coming from the prime nature of the basic aliment or from the strength of the source needs very consistent a wine. After a strong flavour if we want to appreciate also the taste of the wine we need a sample capable of expressing itself at a high taste-aromatic level. It takes a rich and powerful wine with concentrated perfume and taste. Vice versa, not very consistent dishes, delicate, played on light flavours, in order not to be flattened and overwhelmed by the wine, want ethereal wines, not too savoury and not much consistent. The more the course consistency increases the more that of wine should and vice versa.

Therefore there must be absolute harmony between the intensity of the course taste and the intensity of the wine taste.

Equilibrium: in this case it is possible to choose the direction of equilibrating contrast or of emphasising harmony.

A very salty or piquant dish might be linked to a soft and sweet wine in order to see its saline euphoria mitigated by the wine; or it might be coupled with strongly acid a wine so that to emphasise with the wine the savoury strength of the preparation.

With equilibrating linkage it is possible to register really fabulous contacts of tastes and streams studying personalised linkages between a particular course and a peculiar wine variety.

The second main rule is to respect the gradual consistency progression in courses and wines. Never begin with the stronger dish or wine: the subsequent dishes and wines might not be appreciated due to the strength of the taste of the first course. The good meal is a crescendo of taste-aromatic intensity.

In order to chose the peculiar wine variety capable of recalling fruitiness particularly inclined to marry the taste of the course foreseen on the menu please see the wheels of varietal fruitiness presented on next picture 13.

FOODS AND WINE

Horsd'oeuvre: appetising and stimulating meal openings, if not too consistent, they can nicely be linked to fresh and perfumed wines, white and rosé, better if aromatic or rich in notes of fruit, round more than acid. Best of all the Prosecco and generally speaking the sparklings. Rich horsd'oeuvre want rich wines; meat, cold meats and salami or mushrooms horsd'oeuvre ask for a red wine or a white one but of superior consistency.

First dishes: for all pasta dishes the source is determinant. With tomato, vegetables and pulses whites, rosés, reds of medium body, not bitter. With meat sources the red wine is necessary, the best the one eventually used for cooking. With sources based on fish we go back to whites: a few strong recipes for fish preparation might need a red wine. The potato gnocchi, due to their gummy consistency, find a good marriage with red wines. The broths and the soups want a white wine more or less consistent; if they were made of meat it would be better a red wine. Pasta preparations cooked in the oven, timbales and all-home-made pasta preparation request full-bodied whites or reds. The risotto should be considered just as pasta. So it will be the source to determine this or that linkage. First dish preparations with strong and marked smells want aromatic wines.

Meats: red wines of increasing intensity matching the fatness and the aromatic intensity increase of the source. White meats can be magnificently linked with white wines of superior consistency.

Fish: white wines with the possibility (in case of some more cooked preparations or preparations with a lot of source) of finding a good combination with red wines of medium consistency.

Salami and cold meats: cooked salami want red wine; aged salami: red and rosé, better if sparkling; dried sausages: half-bodied reds and oily whites; ham: soft and persuasive whites.

Eggs: rich and soft white wines not bitter reds. Omelettes: aromatic whites.

Cheese: dairy products and ricotta with whites; cheese with harder paste with more and more concentrated taste, from very oily and soft whites to red wines and also wines growing in sweetness, for sure the most indicated for the linkage with cheese. The savoury and piquant sweetness of cheese finds perfect and very pleasant a marriage with sweet wines.

Salads: no wine if dressed with vinegar or lemon; if with oil only, aromatic whites of medium consistency fit well.

Desserts, cakes and ice creams: sweet wines, both sparkling or not, white or red. Here is important to take care of the right marriage with the right wine-fruit if in the preparation of the dessert there was a particular fruit (for instance, a pineapple tart is to be linked with a Traminer; the pear tart with a White Pinot, etc.). Please look for the most appropriate or the desired linkages the wheels of varietal fruitiness presented on next pages. Oily and very sweet desserts want oily and very sweet wines. Puff pastries and creamy cakes want sweet wines but less extractive.

Fruit: fresh: white wines, soft, sweet, rosé, sparkling, perfect the Moscato d'Asti. Never evolved or aged wines: the freshness of fruit would enhance the non-freshness of wine. Dried fruit: white wines more and more consistent and evolved, up to the red wine together with chestnuts. No wine with fruit salads if not added with sugar: acidity and acetousity do not find as pleasant any marriage with wine.

CHAPTER VII

FRUITINESS AND NOT GRAPINESS

The fruitiness is the qualitative mainstay of any wine: there is no pleasantness, harmony or complexity if a wine, first at the nose, then in the mouth does not give fruit. Do not get any further from this simple and pure thought (just as the uncontaminated fruit on the plant): no fruit, no great wine.

The fruitiness exists only if a wine reveals excellent consistency, equilibrium and integrity, parameters determining its quality: in this case fruitiness is the effect of the technical and sensorial perfection of a wine, the synthesis of its pleasantness and the one thing with its quality.

But why fruitiness and not grapiness?

The analytical composition of grape renders it possible its transformation into an alcoholic stable and pleasant drink. Also other fruits in nature can be fermented but the grape adapts to many kind of climates, it ripens facilely, it is easy to tread and it effortlessly becomes liquid. Besides, it is subject to a fermentation easily checkable and has an excellent ratio between water, sugars, acidity and other extractive substances (such a ratio as to allow the attainment of a drink with a fairly high alcohol content - 10% and more -). For all these reasons grape has become the preferred fruit for the wine production in the Mediterranean area and from here in all over the world. So it can be said that in nature there is no other fruit more suitable to the transformation into an alcoholic drink.

Man was clever in individuating and rendering fruitful (this linguistic reference to fruit does not seem casual) this natural grape predisposition compared with that of other fruits.

But the nature, being perfect and non-perfectible, is always complete in anyone of its productive effects, direct and indirect, prime or secondary. Having to privilege one vegetable genus more than others for a certain kind of transformation, the nature primarily perfects the predisposition of such a genus to be transformed, secondarily the nature perfects the result obtainable from this transformation. Therefore grape is the ideal medium to be transformed into a drink whose taste does not represent it only, but also the entire vegetable park of fruits.

One for all and all in one.

The wine, with its majestic alcoholic vector (to which the expressive strength and the slow and progressive perishability of the drink are due) is therefore the transformation product of a fruit. Thanks to this fruit – the grape - each one and also the sum of all the natural fruity pomes - with their burden of infinitely pleasant sensations - are enjoyable in one liquid solution.

And it is even more non-perfectible the fact that the diverse species of the genus grape offer to human sensitiveness the extraordinarily varied and diversified combinations of the recall to the fruity kingdom.

It is natural if the whole of this is touching, yearning and stirring just as wine is; here it is then the fruitiness and not the grapiness.

FRUITINESS AND GRAPE VARIETY

Very many grape varieties exist. Every one characterised by its capability of recalling the constituent fruit, the grape, together with a timbre of one or more fruits diverse from grape, with a recognisable and characteristic aroma. White grape recalls white fruits, the red red fruits. The grape with a timbre of banana, peach and apricot for determined variety of white grapes. Grape with a timbre of blackberry, strawberry, blackcurrant for determined red varieties. It is obvious that such a different shade peculiar of each variety – this is why by the technical jargon it is called "varietal" – is presented in an excellent way and thus in a very recognisable way only by a perfect fruit (excellently consistent, balanced and integral) then transformed into a perfect wine (excellently consistent, balanced and integral).

Wine-fruit exalts the varietal aspect and the pleasant differences: tonal timbres of different fruitiness that offer experiences of infinitely varied linkages with aliments and can magnificently satisfy the sensorial desire of experimenting the suasiveness of a certain fruit in a certain moment. One can long the appreciation of a wine-fruit with pear suggestions; one can desire the caress of a raspberry wine-fruit or that of an apricot wine-fruit. So let's just chose the preferred pome, the one that best meets with the taste-aromatic atmosphere you may love to feel in certain circumstances. Often wines of diverse varieties do not recall only the fruit characteristic of those varieties, that is the characteristic of the reference fruit, but also other fruits, of reference of other varieties. So it may often happen that a Chardonnay does not recall banana only, but banana with pear (generally White Pinot reference fruit), or banana, pear and apricot, Riesling reference fruit. Multivaried fruitiness or fruitiness arch that is direct function of wine consistency and also magnificent merit of any champion. The fruitiness wheels reproduced on next page (Pic. 13) with the indication of the reference fruits of each variety should therefore be considered as a synthesis of the most recurring coupling s. For what observed on former paragraph, any grape variety naturally can present an analogy with any existing fruit.

Wheel of the white fruitiness of wine

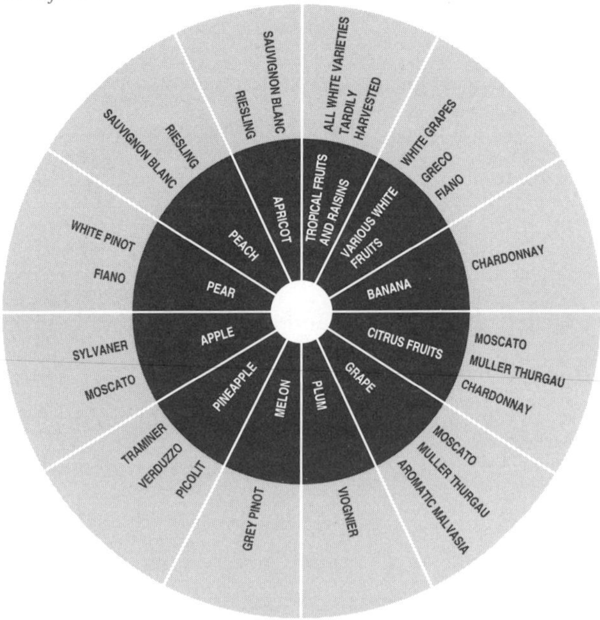

Wheel of the red fruitiness of wine

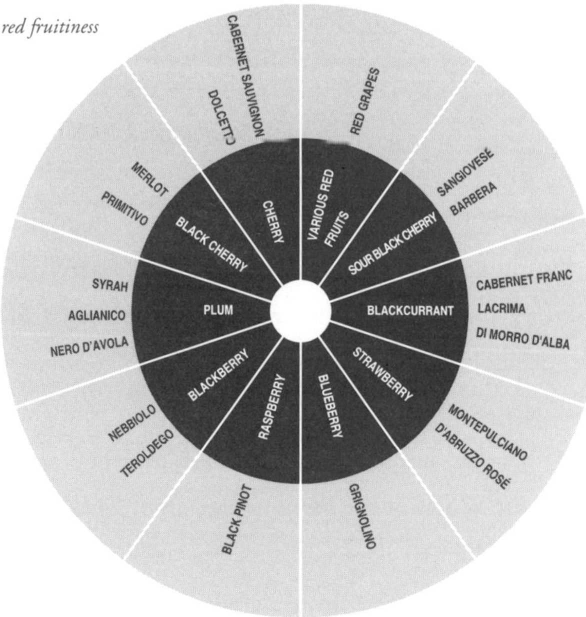

Picture 13

RECALLS AND DIFFERENT ANALOGIES

The analogy or the analogical recall is the relationship of similarity among the perfumes and/or the taste of a wine and the perfumes and/or the taste of another aliment or known element. In other words, the spontaneous identification of the perfume proposed by the wine and that known and memorised of an aliment or element diverse from the wine itself. In substance, the analogy has relevance and can be quoted only if proposed by the wine in an evident and clear way. So, an immediate recall easily perceived and individuated by the taster and not looked for or imposed by him. Analogies of the perfumes and the taste of a wine with grape, ripen fruits, diverse aliments (coffee, cocoa, butter, etc.), with flowers, spices, herbs, minerals, animal smells and with everything else might be revealed during tasting. For instance, the analogy with banana is signalled to indicate the confirmation of an olfactory or gustative sensation similar to that proposed by the mentioned fruit.

It is ridiculous and senseless trying to look for rare analogies proposed by a wine. Who defines a wine only by listing the strangest perfumes evoked by it shows not to know the technique of performing a significant tasting. Differently from the recollection to diverse fruits presented by each grape variety, the analogy is not necessarily a merit. Valuable is the recall to a fruit, not valuable, therefore defective and faulty, is the recall to the sulphureous, to the chemical, to any entity not proper of the constituent grape.

The possible analogies are practically infinite and they are graphically summarised by the Wheel of the Perfumes are after reproduced (Pic. 14). The key of the graphic: 10 classes of principal smells are divided into 28 subclasses, giving place to 153 diverse analogical recalls, mentioned on the external circle of the Wheel of Wine Perfumes. The 10 classes of fundamental smells are fruity, spicy, floral, and ligneous, of positive nature. Of negative nature: microbiological, oxidised, chemical, earthy, vegetal, and tannic.

Wheel of the wine perfumes

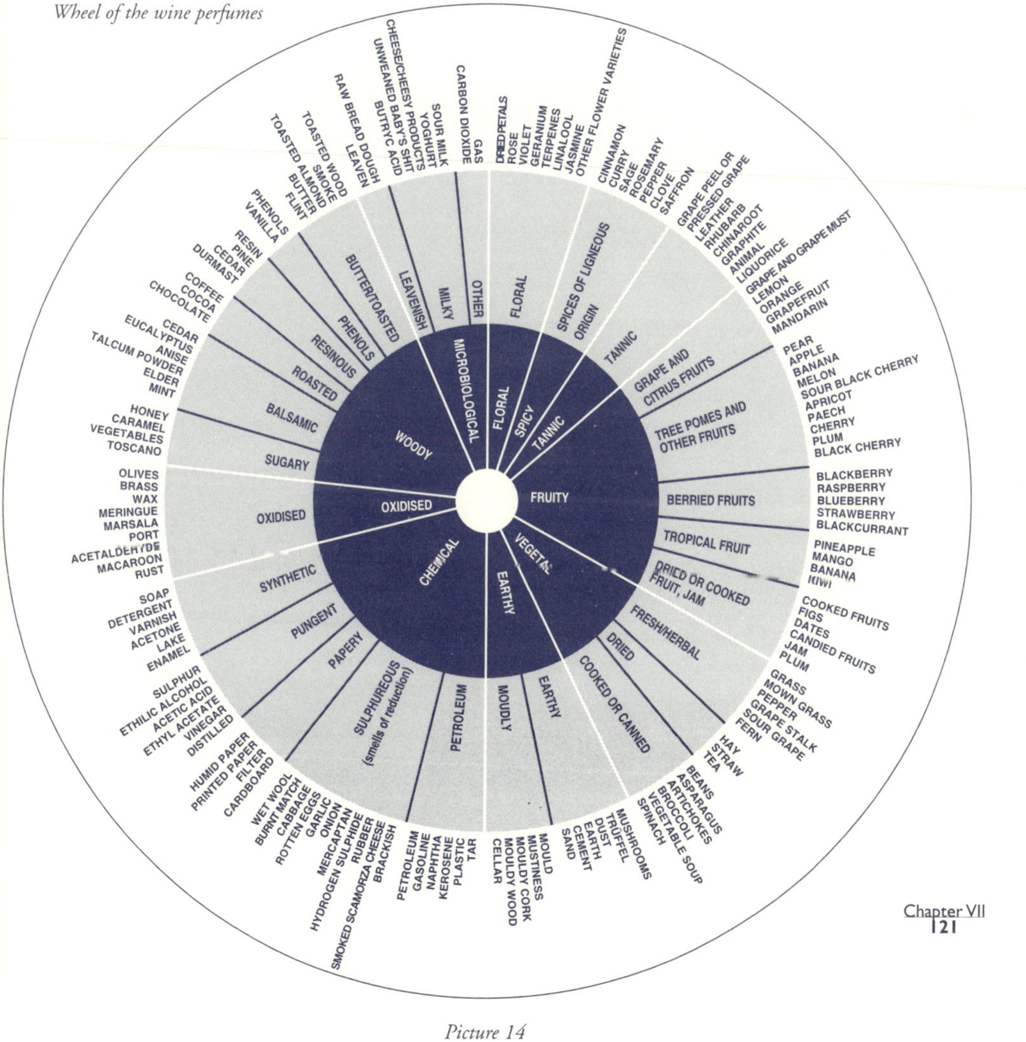

Picture 14

CAPITOLO VIII

OTHER INDEXES OF QUALITY OF WINE

Besides the fundamental Index of Pleasantness-Quality (IP), unique and true measure of the analytical-sensorial value of a wine, there exist other qualitative indexes important for the composition of the final judgement on a given product, on the producer's overall operative talents, on the opportunity of the actual purchase of the examined wine.

THE INDEX VP: VALUE-PRICE INDEX

The Value-Price Index (symbol VP) expresses the relation between the Index of Pleasantness (PI) and the Retail Price (RP) referred to a 0,75 litre bottle: a true Index of Convenience. It is a scalar quantity, of intensive type, measured on a decimal scale. The VP Index increases at the increase of the Index of Pleasantness and decreases at increase of Retail Price (RP). A wine having sufficient Index of Pleasantness (IP = 60) has a sufficient VP (VP = 6) if it is sold at a price below € 5,16 (Lit. 10.000). A wine having Index of Pleasantness worth wine-fruit (IP = 84) has a sufficient VP (VP = 6) if it is sold below € 38,73 (Lit. 75.000).

THE INDEX QQ: QUALITY-QUANTITY INDEX

This index expresses the relation between the Index of Pleasantness (IP) and the number of Bottles in which that wine is produced (nB). A real and true Index of availability and/or diffusion of any wine; a precious indication on the quantitative or specific pleasantness, a measure of each producer's capability of developing a high organoleptical quality on a high number of bottles. This is an index with regards to which Italian wine can and must improve. It is a scalar quantity, of intensive type, measured on a decimal

scale. The QQ Index increases both with the increase of the Index of Pleasantness and the increase of number of Bottles produced.
A wine having sufficient Index of Pleasantness (IP = 60) has a sufficient QQ (QQ = 6) if it is produced in at least 60.000 bottles. A wine having Index of Pleasantness worth wine-fruit (IP = 84) has a sufficient QQ (QQ = 6) if it is produced in at least 3.000 bottles.

THE INDEX QTQ: QUALITY-TOTAL QUANTITY INDEX

For each producer the Index of Quality-Total Quantity (symbol QTQ) expresses the relation between the Average Index of Pleasantness (AIP) of a certain producer and the Total number of Bottles (TnB) realised. It is a true Index of productive capability both in quality and in quantity terms; a precious indication on total quantitative pleasantness or specific total pleasantness. It is a scalar quantity, of intensive type, measured on a decimal scale. The QTQ Index increases both with the increase of the Average Index of Pleasantness of a certain producer and the increase of Total number of Bottles produced.
With Total number of Bottles is meant the algebraic sum of produced bottles of the sole definitive tasted wines. A producer having a sufficient Average Index of Pleasantness (AIP = 60) has a sufficient QTQ Index (QTQ = 6) if he produces at least 1.000.000 bottles. A producer having an Average Index of Pleasantness worth wine-fruit (AIP = 84) has a sufficient QTQ (QQ = 6) if he produces at least 50.000 bottles.

THE INDEX PUR: PURCHASABILITY INDEX

This index (PUR) expresses the relation between the Index of Pleasantness (IP), the Retail Price (RP) referred to a 0,75 litre bottle and the number of Bottles (nB) in which that wine is produced.
It is an overall Purchasability index, referred to pure quality (IP), to convenience (RP), to availability and/or diffusion of any wine (QQ); a precious indication on the possibility of purchasing a worthy and valuable wine. It is a scalar quantity, of intensive type, measured on a decimal scale. The PUR Index increases with the increase of the Index of Pleasantness, decreases at increase of Retail Price and increases at the increase of number of bottles produced.
A wine having a sufficient Index of Pleasantness (IP = 60) has a sufficient PUR Index (PUR = 6) if it is sold at a price below € 5,16 (Lit. 10.000) and if it is produced in at least 60.000 bottles. A wine having an Index of Pleasantness worth wine-fruit (IP = 84) has a sufficient PUR (PUR = 6) if it is sold below € 38,73 (Lit. 75.000) and is produced in at least 3.000 bottles.

MEANING OF TECHNICAL TERMS OF WINE AND TASTING

The glossary of Wine and of Tasting

THE GLOSSARY OF WINE AND OF TASTING

In order to describe and understand the sensations registrable during wine tasting it is useful to know the significance of most recurrent exemplifying terms.

Essential terms are written in italic.

A

Acescence: odour or taste recalling vinegar mainly present in wines with high tenor of volatile acidity or ethyl acetate; synonym of acetous, very grave a defect.

Acetonic: neologism; odour or taste recalling acetone (mainly present in acid wines, in wines fermented in a difficult manner, in re-fermented wines).

Acetous: odour or taste recalling vinegar (mainly present in wines with high tenor of volatile acidity or ethilic acetate); synonym of sourness, severe defect.

Acid: wine with excessive acidity, with not balanced smell and/or taste, sour, raw, sharp and pointed; grave a defect, implicating non complexity and unpleasantness of wine taste.

Acrid: wine presenting olfactory and gustative sensations excessively acid, of unripe fruit; grave a defect; synonym of hard, raw, dry and green; acrid wine is not balanced and therefore it is not complex but simply dominated by sourness.

After (the) mouth: the phase of the tasting subsequent to wine deglutition, in which the sensations of persistency are estimated; synonym of final.

Aggressive: wine striking olfactory or gustative receptors with violent, excessive, pointed sensations, generated by a predominance of acidity and/or bitterness; it is a grave defect because an aggressive wine does not have balanced perfumes and tastes, unpleasant because not soft enough.

Airy: light wine, not much concentrated and/or rich in alcohol; synonym of ethereal and volatile.

Alcoholic fermentation: process of transformation of the sugars into ethilic alcohol and carbon dioxide; the leavens are the agents of the transformation.

Analogical recalls or recall: evident analogy proposed by the perfumes, the taste and the "after mouth" of a wine with fruits, flowers or diverse substances.

Analogy: evident recall proposed by the perfumes, the taste and the "after mouth" of a wine with flowers, fruits or diverse substances; synonym of recollection/recall.

Anhydride sulphurous (So2): substance utilised during vinification; when present in excess it generates a piquant sensation, burning on the nostrils.

Antibotrytics: treatments against mould practised on the fruit in the vineyard (see Botrytis).

Antioidia: treatments against mildew practised on the fruit in the vineyard.

Ampelography: discipline describing and classifying vines from the point of view of their external morphology (buds, leaves, bunches, acinus).

Aromatic bonus: fraction of aromas (spicy, toasted, and balsamic) derived from the elevation wood.

Assembly: mixture/blend of several wines or grapes in order to obtain a unique blending; synonym of blend and cuvée.

Astringent: arid and wrinkled a taste generated by wines rich in tannin; the astringent wine leaves the mouth dried due to the abnormal precipitation of saliva inducted by overabundant tannins.

Astringency: chemical phenomenon generated by wine tannins (substances capable of precipitating immediately the colloidal proteins of saliva) consisting in the diminution of the lubrication of the buccal cavity.

Austere: alcoholic and/or not much sweet a wine, generally characterised by dried acidity, pronounced tannic (bitter) component and by warm taste.

B

Balanced: wine presenting the fundamental gustative stimulus (acidity and softness for white wines; acidity, softness and tannicity for red wines) in perfect reciprocal equilibrium. Synonym of harmonic and "in equilibrium"; augmentative a merit.

Balsamic: odour or taste recalling the fragrance of mint, of eucalyptus, chlorophyll, of toothpaste aromas, recurrent in wines ripened in new oak; qualifying a note when not prevailing on the basic fruit.

Barrique: 225 litres oak barrel, traditionally used in the Bordeaux region.

Beige: particular chromatic tone, between white and straw yellow, presented by white wines of medium concentration.

Big: wine with a superior extractive consistency, body and structure, a big wine is rich in perfumes and has a viscous touch.

Black berry: analogical recall to black-berried wood fruits as blackcurrants, blackberry, blueberry, etc. offered by red wines particularly soft and rich in tannin, tendentially opaque with shades of burgundy-blackish hue.

Bleeding: oenological practise to concentrate extractive substances in the must of red wines. It consists in subtracting from the whole must-wine a liquid part of the compound, thus diminishing the liquid quantity at contact with the solid parts, the peels.

Blend: mixture of several wines or grapes in order to obtain a unique blending; synonym of assembly or mix.

Boisé: taste and savour of vanilla, spices and mint deriving to a wine from its maturation in new or clean durmast barrels; an aromatic bonus (see) that brings in a pleasant – because sweet – additional dimension. When of balanced intensity with respect to the original fruit, it enriches the organoleptic profile of a wine.

Bordeaux mixture: mixture of copper sulphate and slaked lime given to the vine in order to protect it from animal and vegetal parasites; product that sprayed on vines during summer gives the vineyard a characteristic greenish-blue colour.

Botrytis: vegetal parasite (fungus) feeding on water present in the acinus. Fateful when it strikes green grapes, when affecting mature grapes under certain climatic conditions it might produce a beneficial concentration of extractive substances of acinus.

Brassy: neologism, odour or taste recalling brass that renders wine less clean, generally proposed by wines which had non optimal fermentation.

Brut: it indicates a sparkling wine nearly free of residual sugars.

Buffer (to): the mitigating effect on the sensation of acidity or tannicity operated by saliva and extractive substances with sweet taste (see buffer power).

Buffer power: system of protection of pH stability with which any wine is naturally endowed. Calculated through titration of the alkalinity of cinders - protecting with variable intensity the immutability of the acidity strength also under the sensorial point of view - it is one of the factor that determines the acid performance of a wine.

Burning: said of pseudocaloric sensation generated during deglutition by a wine presenting a high tenor of volatile acidity or of ethyl acetate (almost always it is accompanied by stimulus of acescence and sourness), grave a defect.

Burnt: particular smell or taste recalling the characteristic of burnt wood or smoke, deriving to wine from the presence of contaminating substances with sulphureous taste-aroma, or, more rarely, from the elevation in barrels with superficially carbonised staves, synonym of over toasted (see).

Buttery: odour or taste, but also tactile impression recalling the density of butter. A sensation that comes from the extractive richness and is amplified by the optimal modulation of the acid strength of wine generated by malo-lactic fermentation (see).

C

Carbonic: carbon dioxide, gas responsible of the effervescence of sparkling or champagne like wines; in still wines it generates tension of the perfumes. It is called aromatic vector because its evaporation trails and exalts the smells that are extracted by the gas.

Carbonic maceration: particular method of vinification. It consists on putting entire bunches of harvested grapes inside closed wine vases in an environment saturated with carbon dioxide, thus causing an infra-cellular fermentation inside the acinus.The grapes auto-ferment without being pressed beforehand.This is a technique that can foresee an improvement of the organoleptical characteristics of the product, given the exalting of the fruity character subsequent to the brevity and the naturalness of the productive cycle.

Citric: acid coming from the grapes to which is due a sensation of acid freshness recalling the lemon.When in excess it generates the diminution of the salivation with a sour and biting flavour. If used as an adjective it signals an unbalanced wine that due to its excessive acidity presents very intense odours or savours recalling lemon sourness.

Clarification: oenological practise to precipitate some of the constituent substances of wine, thus rendering it more limpid and stabilising it under the proteinic point of view.

Clone: particular subtype of a certain grape variety.There are a few existing clones per any species, more or less productive, quality or quantity wide.

Cheesy: odour or taste recalling cheese; not much qualifying, it is often found in wines that had problems during malolactic fermentation or that have been treated with proteinic substances derived from milk.

Cherry-like: neologism: odour or taste of cherry proposed by red wines with clean and clear fruit; related to the richness in tannins it is an augmentative merit.

Chinaroot: neologism: tendentially bitter odour or taste recalling china, offered by very rich in tannin wines and therefore with perfumes and/or tastes bitterly unbalanced.

Clean: wine devoid of defects and/or extraneous tastes.

Cleanliness: absence in a wine of negative and defective taste aromas improper of the constituent fruit and/or of the correct oenological product of its transformation. The cleanliness is one of the two factors determining the integrity (see); the other one is the newness of the fruit, its non-oxidation.

Cleaving: sharp and angular and penetrating odour or taste, generally referred to wines excessively acid or to wines with too high volatile acidity (see)

Concave: wine nearly devoid of softness, therefore acid (at the entrance into the mouth) and bitter (on the exit) at the same time; very grave a defect because symptom of extreme imbalance.

Configuration: the whole of organoleptical sensations offered by the wine, synonym of implantation.

Connective tissue: the thick and pulpy (fleshy) constituent weft of consistent wines, in fact rare and fluent in diluted ones (it depends on wine richness in extract and in residual of extract - see); synonym of fibre and weft.

Connotation: the complex of the sensorial characteristics determining the fundamental organoleptical features of a wine.

CONSISTENCY: *wine richness in constituent substances. Together with equilibrium and integrity it is one of the three fundamental organoleptical characters, parameters whose intensity determines the index of quality-pleasantness-fruitiness of any wine.*

Constituent fruit: the grape from which a wine is obtained; under a figurative sense it expresses the pureness of the fundamental organoleptical characteristics of the mature acinus on the plant (pulpiness, sweetness and freshness).

Contact: the manner, watery and more or less fluent, with which a wine manifests to the lingual receptors the entity of its consistency; synonym of touch.

Convex: soft wine, rich in ripe and sweet fruit (fragrant entrance, dome of fruit, exit bitter with measure), augmentative a merit, synonym of gustative equilibrium.

Complex: integral and balanced a wine, therefore capable of offering various, multidimensional and qualitative sensations. One defect only or an excess in one of the three fundamental sensations (acidity, bitterness, sweetness) costs this qualifying character.

Cooked: odour or taste of cooked fruit, mainly presented by wines fermented at too high a temperature and partially oxidised. This term is therefore used to signal a scarce fragrance and an evident taste-aromatic heaviness. Recalled cooked fruits are over mature pears by white wines and plums and beetroots by red wines.

Coriaceous: wine with very concentrated tannins, therefore capable of recalling not only the pulp of the constituent fruit, but also the coriaceous grape peel from which the polyphenols are extracted; if not related to an excess of bitter taste it is an augmentative merit.

Corroborant: wine rich in alcohol and extracts therefore with strong and decided perfumes, with a tonic and warm taste.

Creamy: wines with a dense and fat touch, term also used to describe the thickness of the perfumes; merit related to a high consistency.

Crémant: champagne-type wine with fine perlage, characterised by a smaller quantity of carbonic gas and therefore by more plushy, more creamy and less sparkling a touch.

Cryomaceration: in vinification of whites short contact of must with peels at a low temperature to increment the release of substances from the solid parts to the liquid. A risky and potentially counterproductive technique because the induced increase of extract is minimal and it is all based on tannic substances, that is bitter and easily oxidable.

Crystalline: wine so clean to result very brilliant at sight and with uncontaminated perfumes to the taste and the nose, term used to describe exceptionally integral wines.

Cru: defined place of grape production (vineyard).

Cuvée: mixture of more wines or more grapes in order to obtain a unique blending, synonym of blend.

D

Dèbourdage: the becoming limpid of the must.

Decantation: clarification of a wine obtained through the separation of insoluble particles in suspension, it can be natural - sedimentation – or induced through diverse oenological practices.

Decayed: wine whose organoleptical characters have been ruined by an excessive maturation or by an exuberant oxidation; a decayed wine is devoid of fragrance and no more representative of former and original taste-aromatic patrimony of used constituent fruit. Synonym of passed; proper of wines that do not have any potential residual longevity.

Definite: extremely clear and limpid manner with which a fruit is recalled by the perfume or the taste of a wine. Synonym of clean, with an even more qualifying meaning, it is a term used to describe wines with high integrity.

Definition: cleanliness and clearness character, proper of a wine with taste-aromatic contours devoid of any blurring, qualifying a merit and synonym of cleanliness and integrity.

Deglutition: moment in which wine is swallowed. If during this phase an acetous vibration or a tickle or a rustic taste are perceived it means that acetous or sulphureous vices compromise the integrity of wine.

Dégorgement: in sparkling wines obtained through champenois method is an operation consisting in separating residuals of second fermentation (dregs and dead leavens) that took place in the bottle from wine.

Degree: alcoholic degree.

Dense: wine with a dense and fat touch (also used to describe the thickness of perfumes); augmentative merit.

Disk (wine disk): the round surface of wine inside glass as seen from the top.

Dirty: not clean wine, presenting odours or tastes extraneous to those of fruit, originated by an improper vinification, synonym of imprecise, very grave defect.

Disguised: wine presenting an excess of ligneous odours or tastes derived from the oak elevation.

Dismature: neologism, sour odour or taste, green and unripe, it is said of a wine presenting an excess in acidity; grave a defect of the equilibrium.

Disposition: this term expresses the manner in which the odour or the taste of a wine is arranged with respect to the softness and/or the acidity; in other words with respect of the sensation of ripeness of the fruit. A wine is well disposed when it is soft, badly disposed when it is acid or overmatured; well-disposed wines are balanced and not vice versa.

Dregs: slimy and more or less gross residuals of fermentation (dead leavens); wine contacting these parts looses integrity (cleanliness of perfumes) and equilibrium of savour (bitterness increases).

Drinkable: neologism, said of a wine with pleasant, moved and spontaneous drinkability.

Dry: wine presenting a hard, dried, bitterish, nearly devoid of softness odour or taste, or presenting a note more acid bitter than soft, proper of wines excessively acid. Grave a defect, no other word used to describe organoleptical characteristics of wine ever produced more damages than the term dry. In fact a dry wine is a wine with a taste unpleasantly acid-bitter, the tasting of which does not generate any kind of pleasure. It is then fundamental to spread the concept that any wine should reveal a fraction of convenient sweetness (see) to recall the indispensable suasiveness of the ripe fruit on the vine.

During (the) mouth: the gustative phase of tasting, corresponding to the transit of wine in the buccal cavity.

E

Earthiness: tactile sensation of fibrousness, proper of wines very rich in tannin, with thick and dense internal touch.

Edge disk: the circular edge of the wine surface close to the face of the glass; synonym of nail.

Edible: analogical term to indicate a wine extremely rich in extracts, with very thick internal touch (see), with a pulpy and fibrous tactile profile, nearly "solid-like"; sensation proposed by exceptionally consistent wines; synonym of masticable.

Entrance: odour or taste that opens the olfactory or the gustative phase.

EQUILIBRIUM: *organoleptical character that provides for the balancing of the perfumes and of the tastes of a wine among acid, sweet and bitter sensations. A wine is balanced when its taste is as soft as acid-bitter. A wine is balanced when the Sweet Taste Sensations are equal to the sum of Acid Taste Sensations + Bitter Taste Sensations (Eq = STS = ATS + BTS). Together with consistency and integrity it is one of the three fundamental organoleptical characters, parameters the intensity of which determine the index of quality-pleasantness-fruitiness of any wine.*

Ethereal: wine rich in alcohol, not much extractive, light and femininely connoted, synonym of airy and volatile.

Excess: superabundance of a specified substance.

Expressive volume: intensity with which a wine offers to the examination of senses the whole of the perfumes and the tastes with which it is endowed (high in wines rich in extracts and alcohol, low in the inconsistent ones).

Extract: the total dried extract of a wine, also said body of the wine, is the whole of the wine constitutive components, water, alcohol and volatile agents excluded. It is obtained by subjecting to evaporation the volatile substances of wine, that is why it corresponds to the weight of the fixed remnants measured in grams per litre (g/l); the extract is in substance the chemical-physical agent of the consistency of wine.

Extractive: wine rich in extracts, therefore thick and consistent.

Extract remains: all the extractive substances diverse from acids, mainly with sweet taste (glycerine, pectic substances, gummy, mucilaginous, etc.), the most precious extract: the pulp of grapes.

F

Fatness: sensation of superior richness and olfactory and/or gustative softness proper of consistent and mature wines, augmentative a merit.

Feeble: wine whose organoleptical characters are weak or not balanced due to its low acidity; synonym of weak or seated.

Feminine: light wine, not much rich in extracts, delicate clean and ethereal; the aspect of a wine femininely connoted is tendentially transparent, the perfumes are unsubstantial, the structure is not imposing, the touch is light and the constitutive weft rather sparse.

Fibre: the intimate consistency of a wine, that is its capability of recalling the pulp of the fruit, the grape, thanks to its richness in extracts; synonym of intimate connective tissue and weft, fibrousness determines the internal touch (see) of a wine.

Filtration: clarification of wine through filters (mainly in cardboard).

Final: the whole of the sensations persisting in the mouth after wine deglutition; synonym of closing or exit.

Fleeting: inconsistent wine with a final of scarce persistency, synonym of short, grave defect.

Fleshy: wine rich in extractive substances the intimate connective tissue (see) of which is so thick to give a gustative impression of edible solidity. A fleshy wine is very consistent, of great structure and of dense and fibrous internal touch (see). If not related to a bitter taste, it is an augmentative merit and an organoleptic character proper of great red wines.

Floral: it is said of a clean nose, tendentially soft, but not much concentrated or thick enough to give fruit.

Freshness: newness, absolute fragrance of the taste-aroma presented by the examined wine. Augmentative a merit the presence of which in a wine is inverse function of its degree of oxidation. The more a wine is fresh the more brilliant it results to the senses, the longer its time duration is.

***FRUIT:** central mainstay of the quality of wine and of tasting terminology. Any wine* *must give fruit, must recall the taste-aroma of the grape (or analogously the taste-aroma of other pomes), pulpy and mature on the plant. There is no pleasantness if a wine first to the nose then to the mouth does not give fruit. It is necessary to fix deeply this pure and simple thought. No fruit, no good wine. It is then basic the verification of the fruit presence in a wine: an examination together simple (presence of fruit = pleasantness) and complex (presence of fruit = excellence of wine with respect to the three fundamental organoleptical characters: consistency, equilibrium and integrity; in other words the absence of gaps or analytical - technical defects in examined wine).*

FRUITINESS: *the pleasantness-quality of wine determined by and consisting in the sum of the consistency, the equilibrium and the integrity of the fruit taste-aroma revealed by each wine during tasting.*

Fruity: wine with a high index of technical and analytical quality thanks to the universal pleasantness of the constituent fruit (grape) recalled by its taste, synonym of pleasant and qualitative.

Full: wine rich in extracts and soft that thanks to its consistency and viscosity generates a wide volume of mouth (see).

Fulling: oenological operation consisting in sinking the cap of marcs in the must with the special tools. During the fermentation and the maceration it promotes the cession of extractive substances from the peels. It is a practice potentially positive but when practised in excess it provokes a worsening of the equilibrium of a wine given the excess of bitter tannic substances extracted.

G

Glycerinous: odour or taste of emollient substances offered by very alcoholic wines, rich in glycerine and generally obtained by over mature and/or withered grapes; when referred to the external touch it signals the smoothness of the liquid.

Grape blendings: mixture of grapes of diverse varieties that compounds a wine.

Grapy: odour or taste of a wine that suggests, untouched and uncontaminated, the grapiness of the constituent fruit, mature and pulpy on the plant. It is an augmentative merit and an organoleptic character that should be presented by any wine. Synonym of fruity, with a more specific reference to constituent fruit.

Green: herbal, vegetal sour odour or taste, grave defect.

Gummy: odour or taste recalling the softness of gum, it derives to wines from the richness in extracts, augmentative a merit proper of very consistent wines. It represents a pleasantness increaser if not exuberant with respect to the basic fruitiness.

H

Hard: wine offering excessively acid olfactory and gustative sensations, referring to unripe fruit or excessively bitter sensations; grave defect of equilibrium; synonym of sour, dry and raw.

Harmonic: wine presenting the fundamental gustative stimulus (acidity and softness for white wines; acidity, softness and tannicity for red wines) in perfect reciprocal equilibrium. Compact a nose and a taste but rich in facetings singularly advisable; synonym of balanced and in equilibrium.

He: short for hectare.

Herbaceous: odour or taste recalling grass; defect characteristic of wine obtained by unripe grapes; synonym of vegetal, defect of equilibrium.

I

INTEGRITY: *a wine is integral when its perfumes and taste are clean and new. That is to say when it is devoid of defects and not oxidised and when it offers a recall to the constituent fruit devoid of distortions and interferences (extraneous vices improper of grape), without being at the same time defibrated by orangish, sweetish and/or rancid touches of oxidation. Together with consistency and integrity it is one of the three fundamental organoleptical characters, parame-*

ters whose intensity determines the index of quality-pleasantness-fruitiness of any wine.

Intensity: expressive energy of a wine, an intense wine is that which expresses with strength and vigour its perfumes and taste. It is a variable organoleptical character; the intensity of a wine is direct function of the consistency and the alcoholic degree.

Imprecise: not clean a wine, therefore not integral presenting odours or tastes extraneous to those of the fruit, originated by an improper vinification; synonym of dirty or perturbed. Grave a defect, signifying a problematic vinification.

L

Lacquered: odour or taste of lake for furniture, recurring in wines with acid disposition, elevated in new wood and/or with high volatile acidity.

Lactic: acid originating in wine after malolactic fermentation: the malic acid of grape becomes lactic thanks to the action of malolactic bacteria.

Leathery: neologism: dark and bitter odour or taste recalling leather, offered by wines too rich in tannin and therefore with bitter perfumes and/or taste.

Leavens: unicellular micro-organisms that provoke the alcoholic fermentation.

Lemony: neologism: wine presenting an odour or a taste of sour fruit, sharp and metallic, proper of wines excessively acid, grave a defect of the equilibrium.

Ligneous: neologism, wine presenting excessive odour or taste of wood.

Limpid: referred to the colour, wine with brilliant aspect, devoid of substances in suspension. Referred to the odour or the taste, it expresses the cleanliness of the fruit that is the absence in a wine of vices not proper of grape from which it was originated.

Liquorice: odour or taste recalling that of liquorice, recurrent in red wines contemporaneously over acid and over tannic, analogical recall composed by the convergence of tannin on the lemony acid base.

Long: wine that once swallowed leaves in the mouth persistent and prolonged taste aromatic sensations.

M

Maceration: contact of the must with the solid parts of the bunch (peels) during the vinification of red wines.

Madeirised: odour or taste of sweetish citrus fruit more or less rancid recalling Madeira; character proper of dried wines and therefore not integral that accuse oxidation (see) and that have their own taste-aromatic profile irreversibly degraded.

Malic: acid coming from grapes to which is due a fragrant sensation reinforcing the fruity effect; when in excess it generates a sense of bitterness and immaturity.

Malolactic fermentation: secondary fermentation during which malic acid degrades to lactic acid with effects of modulation of acidity sensation.

Masculine: powerful and structured a wine, rich in alcoholic degree and tannins with a tendentially bitter taste. Wine manfully connoted has a decided coloration resulting not much transparent to the sight.

Massive: wine with superior extractive consistency, rich and structured.

Masticable: analogy to indicate a wine with extreme consistency, with very thick internal touch (see), under certain ways nearly solid; sensation generally proposed by red wines rich in extractive and tannic substances, synonym of edible.

Mature: wine with convenient acidity (not in excess or scarce); in this case it indicates an odour or a taste of a wine soft and full, at the same time sweet and fragrant, augmentative a merit.

Mercaptan (smell of): repulsive odour of organic compound (autolisys of fermentative leavens) that contains sulphur. Mercaptan causes an olfactory perturbation of wine with the subsequent strong sulphureous odour.

Meringue: neologism, odour or taste recalling meringue which renders wine less clean, generally proposed by wines that had a non optimal fermentation.

Mesh: the connective tissue, the fibre in wines, particularly the reds; related to the internal touch, it is thick in wines rich in extracts, sparse in the poor ones, synonym of fibre.

Milkiness: organoleptical character with two meanings. 1) Positive: a tactile sensation of particular creaminess offered by consistent and balanced wines. 2) Negative: flavour of slightly acid milk presented by red wines that had difficult malolactic fermentation.

Milky: terms with two meanings. 1) Positive if referred to the touch: a dense and thick wine with viscous touch and with softly balanced taste. 2) Negative if referred to the taste: wine presenting a non-fragrant flavour due to the presence of notes of more or less rancid milk (yoghurt), anyway not fresh.

Mineral: odour or taste analogously recalling substances like petroleum, iron, naphtha; sensation recurrent in not integral and very acid white wines (particularly from Riesling grapes), it derives to wine from the convergence of the lemony note on the strong smoked sulphureous; grave a defect of the integrity.

Moved: it is said of a balanced and varied taste between the extremes of acid and soft in white wines and acid, soft and tannic in red wines. A wine presenting a moved taste is wide, balanced and complex. It is pleasant.

Mould (noble): see Botrytis, synonym of noble putrefaction.

Mouth: the whole of the gustative sensations of a wine, synonym of palate, taste.

Mute: wine not much expressive, with neutral odour or taste, not much intense, inconsistent wine is mute.

N

Nail: the edge of the wine surface near to the side of the glass, synonym of edge disk.

Narrow: wine excessively acid, with a raw and aggressive taste nearly devoid of sweetness and therefore sharp, acute and never wide, open, grave defect of equilibrium.

Neutral: wine with not much accentuated organoleptical characters with diluted and not much intense odours or tastes; defect originated from the scarce extractive consistency of a wine.

Newness: absence in a wine of oxidised taste aromas not proper of the constituent fruit and/or not proper of the correct oenological product of its transformation. The newness is one of the two factors determining the integrity (see); the other one is the cleanliness of the fruit, its non-dirtiness.

Note: olfactory and/or gustative spur that permits the identification and conditions the liking of a wine.

Nose: the whole of the odorous sensations of a wine.

O

Oenology: discipline and technique related to wine production.

Oidium: vine disease provoked by a small fungus implying the withering of the acinus.

Old-sensations: wine in which evolved and oxidised notes prevail, characteristic of a fruit no more tonic and violaceous but withered and orange-coloured (typical of wines aged in wood for a long time).

Old-style: wine with taste-aromatic nuances of caramelised and passito fruit.

Olfaction: it defines the repeated and prolonged inhalations directed to the individuation of the odorous profile of a wine.

Organoleptical: it designates the qualities or the characteristics referred to a wine that can be perceived and evaluated by the organs of sense during the tasting. For instance the colour, the odour or the taste of the examined sample; synonym of sensorial.

Out of focus: wine presenting not much clean perfumes or gustative notes, thus to render the recall to constituent grape imprecise and with not well definite edges, it represents a defect.

Over mature: referred to a wine lacking in acidity, seated and feeble, it represents an irreversible defect.
Over spicy: neologism, wine presenting excessive odour or taste of spices derived from elevating wood (for instance, saffron, vanilla, cannel, Lebanon cider, etc.).
Over tannic: neologism, wine presenting excessive bitter odour or taste, generated by an excess of tannins causing analogies with leather, rhubarb, liquorice and china.
Over toasted: neologism: wine presenting excessive odour or taste of smoky/toasted derived from sulphureous or from the elevation in oak (for instance, coffee grounds, burnt wood).
Over woody: neologism, wine presenting excessive odour or taste of wood.
Oxidation: gradual and natural degenerative process of the taste-aromatic properties of the constituent substances of wines. During the first phase it produces an accentuation of the sensation of sweetness; at a later stage it turns to more or less controlled acid and in the end it gets to odours or smells which recall Madeira. Oxidised wines have toasted perfumes, almond and Madeira like; an old taste not balanced due to the acid bitter and rancid taste of decayed substances. When it involves a wine at the moment of its introduction into the market it is a grave defect, a defect substantially penalising two of the three fundamental organoleptical characters of a wine: integrity and equilibrium.

P

Palate: the whole of the gustative sensations of a wine, synonym of mouth.
Passed: wine whose organoleptical qualities are irreversibly degenerated due to too long an ageing or to a sudden and precocious oxidation, synonym of decayed.
Passito: passito odour or taste, warm, glycerinous and not much fragrant generally offered by wines obtained from over mature grapes.

Peely: neologism; bitter odour or taste recalling savouriness of the grape skin (rich in tannin); a peely wine is an overtannic wine, therefore too bitter a wine; defect that penalises the gustative equilibrium of wines, especially the red ones.

Perfume: synonym of odour, with a more qualifying meaning.

Perlage: small bubbles of carbon dioxide characteristic of sparkling or champagne like wines.

Persistency: the whole of the taste aromatic sensations remaining in the mouth after wine deglutition.

Perturbed: unclean wine presenting odours or tastes extraneous to the ones of fruit and originated by an improper vinification; synonym of dirty and imprecise, very grave a defect.

pH: pure number indicating the sensorial or the real acidity of a given acidity of titration. pH is the chemical-physical constituent agent of a wine. pH equal to 7 is index of neutrality (water). The high pH of a wine (3,6-3,9) indicates a moderate energy of its acids, that is a contained organoleptical acidity and therefore a good equilibrium of its taste, vice versa for low pH (2,9-3,3).

Phase: the moment of tasting in which wine is subjected to the screening of a particular organ of sense. The tasting is substantiated in the visual, olfactory and gustative phases: the analysis of the manner in which a given wine results to the eye, the nose and the mouth of the taster.

Phylloxera: animal parasite of vines ho, feeding with vine roots causes the death of the plant.

PLEASANTNESS OF THE TASTE: *the quality of wine.*

Picture: term generally utilised to define the whole of the perceived olfactory notes, it can also be extensively and figuratively used to signify the organoleptical complex of the raised sensations: a complex gustative picture, etc., synonym of phase and profile.

Pièce: 228-litre oak barrel, traditionally used in Burgundy.

Piquant: wine presenting rustic, spicy, sulphureous (sulphur, eggs and cheese) taste aromas. Defective notes, dirty, sharp and bitterish that gravely penalise the softness and the fragrance of the fruit to which they are over imposed.

Polymerisation: chemical process through which more molecules of tannin join together with their subsequent precipitation due to the increase of their molecular weight (greater than the original one). In red wines it is a phenomenon typical of the ageing due to which wine progressively clears of its tannic substances. The polymerisation of a wine is direct proportion of its oxidation and the polymerisation of the tannins, taste wise, implies the caramelising of red wine flavour.

Polyphenols: the tannic substances of a wine, the total polyphenols expressed in grams per litre represent the sum of the anthocyans and the tannins.

Potential longevity: possibility of wine of lasting through time, qualifying character depending on consistency and on oxidative integrity of wine.

Power: incisiveness, strength and expressive energy given to wine by its richness in alcohol.

Powerful: wine with high alcoholic content with accentuated aroma and taste with a warm thermic contact.

Press (wine of): vinous liquid resulting from the pressing of the marcs through pneumatic, hydraulic or mechanical press; more precious than wrung wine with respect to which it presents a minor concentration of tannins.

Prime (fruit): uncontaminated fruit with an intact taste aromatic patrimony.

Profile: term used with two meanings. 1) The whole of the sensations, the general trait, the sensorial scene (both olfactory and gustative) which characterises a wine giving the essential data to individuating and describing the general organoleptical structure. 2) The profile might be that supplied by acidity: the nerve, the relief, the shape and the figure given by the acid to the sweet and soft fruit-extractive mass.

Project (to): to announce, to tell in advance; term generally used to indicate the olfactory and gustative expectations generated by the visual examination or the gustative ones generated by olfactory scrutiny.

Propellant: the alcohol that conducts and supports with energy the odours and the tastes of a wine.

Pseudocaloric: impression of warmth generating from the contact of a wine very much endowed with alcohol and the lingual papilla; thermic relief proportional to the strength of the alcoholic content.

Pulpiness: odorous or tactile a sensation of fleshy consistency, it is proper of soft and rich in extracts wines, augmentative a merit.

Pulpy: it is said of perfume or taste thick and dense endowed with pulpiness (see); character that is the reflection of the thick and doughy consistency of a wine, augmentative a merit.

R

Rancid: odour or taste of acid-bitter tendency recalling toasted almond, macaroon and slightly sour butter. An organoleptical character proper of partially oxidised and older wines, therefore not integral, that begin to accuse oxidation (see) and that due to this have their taste aromatic profile irreversibly degraded; sensorial defect with gravity proportional to intensity.

Raw: aggressive, cold and metallic odour or taste, it is said of a wine presenting an excess in acidity, grave defect in equilibrium.

Recall or analogical recall: evident analogy proposed by the perfumes, the taste and the after mouth of a wine with fruits, flowers or diverse substances.

Receptors: the organs of sense that has receptive capability or function. For instance, the gustative receptors are the papilla that contacted by wine register stimuli immediately sent to the brain and by this interpreted as index of extractive consistency-viscosity of examined wine.

Red berry: analogical recall to red-berried wood fruits, as raspberry, strawberry, sour black cherry, etc., offered by red wines not much concentrated in tannin and therefore of a ruby red colour brilliant and transparent.

Reduction: physical chemical state of wine during the phases of productive process; it indicates the stay of a wine in anaerobic environment, that is not in contact with air.

Redundant: exuberant odour or taste and therefore gushy; it compromises equilibrium and therefore the taste aromatic complexity of a wine. Generally it is the sweetness of an over mature fruit or just oxidised one to be redundant, it represents a defect.

Refinement: wine stabilisation in glass or inside containers in other material (wood, steel, cement, etc.); an excessive refinement generates the oxidation of the product that is the diminution of its integrity.

Refrigeration: stabilisation and clarification of must and/or wine (precipitation of tartaric substances in suspension) obtained through drastic fall in temperature.

Remains (of extract): all the extractive substances diverse from acids, mainly with sweet taste (glycerine, pectic substances, gummy, mucilaginous, etc.), the most precious extract: the pulp of grapes.

Repassing: it consists in renewing the liquid through pumping it at contact with the grape dregs. It is an oenological practice that generates a greater cession of substances from the peels. If repassed in excess a wine can present a non-balanced taste due to an excess of tannic substances.

Reducing sugars: non-fermentable sugary substances present in balanced wines (white and red) nearly at the level of traces (0-2 grams per litre).

Residuals (sugary): sugary substances present in sweet wines or in a smaller quantity in the balanced ones, synonym of residual sugars.

Resinous: odour or taste recalling resin and recurrent in wines with acid disposition, with high volatile acidity and elevated in new wood; defect

Ripe: wine with convenient acidity (not in excess or scarce); in this case it indicates an odour or a taste of a wine soft and full, at the same time sweet and fragrant, augmentative a merit.

Rootstock: due to the devastating Phylloxera's attacks of last century and seen the vulnerability of the roots of the European species with reference to this parasite, vines are not planted directly in the ground. They are inter-grafted on supports of American origins called rootstocks, resistant to the attacks of Phylloxera.

Round: said of a balanced wine, soft, mature always harmonically various in the proposed sensations and therefore complex a wine.

Rustic: rough odour or taste, presented by wines disturbed with sulphureous notes; defect.

S

Sample: examined wine.

Short: wine scarcely persistent, due to its inconsistency, synonym of fleeting, very grave a defect.

Seated: referred to a wine scarce in acidity, over mature and feeble; grave and irreversible a defect.

Sensorial: it designates the qualities or the properties related to a wine that can be perceived and evaluated by the organs of sense during tasting, for instance the colour, the odour and the taste of the examined sample; synonym of organoleptic.

Severe: wine with close odour or taste, not balanced, nor wide or sweet, of a bitter taste-olfactory tendency because generally too rich in tannin; synonym of austere.

Sizing: operation of clarification realised with a product (egg albumen, fish-glue, gelatine, etc.) that precipitates the roughest suspended particles.

Slim: wine scarce in extracts and alcohol, watery and poor with slender structure and fleeting final.

Sour: raw odour or taste, of green or lemony gustative tendency; attributed to a wine presenting an excess of acidity; heavy a defect in the equilibrium of taste, due to a non complete maturation of constituent grape.

Sour milk: odour or taste of acid milk and of yoghurt generally related to problems of vinification.

Smoked: piquant perfume and taste, dark, tendentially bitter proposed by wines whose fruit is covered by sulphureous (see).

Smoky: odour or taste of smoke generated by sulphureous contamination or by smoked wood (by fire of other kind of wood), a bitter note that implies a diminution of the gustative equilibrium of wine.

Smooth: wine the contact of which with gustative receptors (lingual papilla) is balanced and therefore caressing; an external touch (see) generating a pleasant sensation of softness which is originated by the conspicuous quantity of glycerine in wine.

Soapy: wine at the beginning of the oxidative process, scarcely endowed with acidity, the fruitiness of which presents chemical and sweetish tones of soaps and cosmetics.

Soft: wine presenting a sensation of fruit appropriately mature, tendentially sweet but also fragrant (fairly acid). Augmentative a merit, the softness of a wine signals the equilibrium of its taste, in fact if a fat wine is always soft, a soft wine might not be fat.

Souplesse: softness and plushy touch characteristic of wines balanced because obtained from completely mature grapes; augmentative merit.

Spicy: odour or taste of spices deriving to wine from the elevating wood (for instance, cannel, vanilla, tea, saffron, etc,).

Stabilisation: any oenological treatment to eliminate from wine before bottling any micro-organisms capable of causing a new and undesired fermentation or precipitation; three are the existing types of stabilisation: micro biological, tartaric and proteic.

Structure: the whole of the organoleptical sensations revealed by the examined wine, the whole of the constitutive elements of a wine, synonym of configuration.

Structured: strong wine, rich in alcohol and in extractive substances, well concentrated at the nose and the mouth because superiorly endowed with consistency.

Suasiveness: character proper of a balanced and soft wine that expresses the smoothness of its touch and the tendential sweetness of its perfumes and taste, augmentative merit.

Sugars (reducing): non-fermentable sugary substances present in balanced wines (white and red) nearly at the level of traces (0-2 grams per litre).

Sugars (residuals): sugary substances present in sweet wines or in smaller quantity in balanced wines.

Sugary: odour or taste of the evolution that can involve both sweet and non sweet wines. In fact sugars candy but also the tannins of the old red wines with orange or brick red chromatic reflections (polymerisation of tannins = sugary flavour of their taste-aromas); a sugary red wine is a wine more or less oxidised.

Sulphureous: wine presenting rustic, piquant, sulphureous (sulphur, eggs and cheese) taste aromas, deriving to wine from improper vinification (mainly due to non-optimal fermentations and to late or insufficient decantings). Defective notes, dirty, sharp and bitterish that gravely penalise the softness and the fragrance of the fruit to which they are over imposed. Grave defect, irreversible vice and of differently increasing intensity after bottling, it perturbs cleanliness (and therefore integrity) unfortunately quite often recurrent.

Sulphurous anhydride (So2): substance utilised during vinification that when present in excess generates a piquant sensation, burning on the nostrils.

Sweet: soft and mature for white and red wines, sugary for the sweet ones.

Sweetness: diverse from the merely sugary sensation, this is a term of fundamental importance used to express the softness, the maturity, the acidity and bitterness of a wine when not in excess. It is an absolute merit because wines must not be dry or green and seen the fact that a wine cannot be pleasant (quality wide) if devoid of a portion of the same gustative sweetness that characterises the fruit on the plant.

Synthetic: unnatural odour or taste, desiccating and evoking chemical substances like varnish, enamel and diluents generally related to high tenor of volatile acidity or presented by very acid wines elevated in new wood.

T

Talcum powder/talcum powdery: neologism: odour and more rarely taste of sweet tendency, recalling talcum powder and presented by pulpy and mature white wines.

Tannic: odour or taste of bitter and peely tendency generated by polyphenolic substances. When in exuberance tannin generates sensations that render bitter the perfume and the taste of wine. It is a grave defect because the exuberance of bitterness, agent of gustative unpleasantness, is the strongest deterrent to the appreciation of wine qualities.

Tartaric: acid coming from grapes to which is due an acid sensation tendentially hard, in excess it generates burning and aggressive flavour.

Tasting: technical and methodical evaluation of the index of quality-pleasantness-fruitiness of wine; the attentive perception of the nature and the intensity of the sensations generated by the chemical-physical wine components in the person who enters in contact with it; synonym of sampling.

Tensive: neologism, effect of tension of perfumes and taste produced by exuberant relief of alcoholic content, and/or acidity, and/or carbon dioxide.

Thick: it expresses the concentration of extractive substances that gives wine a dense tactile thickness; thick is the wine with high consistency.

Thinning out (of bunches of grapes): elimination of some bunches from a vine, before final period of maturation in order to concentrate juice in a smaller number of acinus; a technique inducing a greater extractive consistency.

Threadbare: evolved wine, moderately oxidised that due to the ageing has orange colour, waxy taste and moderate spurs of fruitiness, scarce potential residual longevity.

Tight: not relaxed odour or taste (nose or palate) due to an excess of acidity or alcoholic content.

Toasted: smoky odour or taste deriving to wine from sulphureous defect or from elevating wood excessively burnt (for instance, torrefaction notes, cocoa, coffee, burnt gun, etc.).

Touch: sensation of density or fluency generated by contact of wine with lingual papilla; the viscosity of wine touch increases at increase of wine consistency.

Touch – external: tactile sensation limited to the sole quality of the contact of wine with lingual receptors. It is related with the richness in extract, particularly in glycerine. The wine with a good external touch caresses plushy, smooth, viscous; that lacking in external touch results fluid and watery.

Touch – internal: tactile sensation referred to the fibre, to the intimate connective tissue of wine. It is related to the richness in residual of extract (see) and in tannins. The wine with good internal touch results pulpy and fleshy; that lacking of internal touch slips mastication and creates a scarce volume in the mouth.

Traction: particular effect generated by carbon dioxide and alcohol consisting in pulling and trailing the perfumes of a wine toward the olfactory receptors.

Truncated: wine with a sudden final incapable of offering any persistency, grave defect recurrent in wine lacking of consistency.

U

Unripe: wine presenting hard, dried and raw taste – aromas, grave defect of gustative equilibrium due to the usage of sour fruits; it does not decrease even with a more prolonged maturation in glass (refinement).

V

Vanished: two the meanings. 1) Redundant odour, sweetish, of oxidised alcohol. 2) Wine with organoleptical characteristics degraded by excessive maturity or by incipient oxidation.

Varietal: odour or taste characteristic of the grape species from which wine is obtained.

Variety: species of grape.

Varnish: unnatural odour or taste desiccating and evoking chemical substances like enamels and diluents, generally related to an high tenor of volatile acidity or to very acid wines elevated in new wood.

Vector: this term individuates the organoleptical parameters responsible of the taste-aromatic energy of a wine; alcohol and carbon dioxide, if present, are fundamental vectors.

Vegetal: odour or taste recalling the vegetation, proper of not completely mature wine. Synonym of herbal, grave defect of equilibrium due to exuberant acidity.

Verve: acid fragrance.

Vibrant, vibrating: high frequency organoleptical note, of acetous matrix, which lets the perceived taste or perfume vibrate; which makes the wine vibrate on the uvula at the moment of deglutition. Defect that takes away suasiveness and fragrance and renders wine taste similar to the one of distilled (like grappa, cognac, whisky, etc.); generally proposed by old wines and/or improperly vinified and aged in wood.

Vinous: inelegant odour or taste presented by wines scarce in integrity and poor in alcoholic content, it represents a defect.

Vintage: year of harvesting.

Virile: powerful and structured wine, of masculine connotation (see) rich in alcoholic content and tannins, of a taste tendentially unbalanced due to exuberant bitterness.

Viscosity: dense and thick tactile sensation, not watery generated by very consistent wines.

Volatile: light wine, not much extractive, feminine, generally with alcohol in isolated evidence, synonym of airy and ethereal.

Volatile acidity: chemical wine component measured in acetic acid. When in excess it produces an unnatural and acetous smell (varnish), a vibrant taste, turning sour, bitterish and a burning deglutition. When present in concentrations not elevated to the point of causing the above described defective impressions, it originates a drying process and a stinging persistency that attenuates the softness and the taste-aromatic fragrance of a wine.

Volume (expressive): intensity with which a wine offers to the examination of senses the whole of perfumes and tastes with which it is endowed (high in wines rich in extracts and alcohol, low in the inconsistent ones).

W

Warm: it is said of a wine that due to its richness in alcohol gives an olfactory or gustative impression of heat.

Waxy: odour or taste recalling wax offered by very alcoholic wines, rich in glycerine and generally obtained by over mature and/or withered grapes. Waxy wine is warm, externally smooth but not fat under the tactile point of view because slippery: it has a good external (see) but not internal (see) touch.

Weft: see fibre and intimate connective tissue.

Wide: wine presenting perfumes and gustative stimulus balanced amongst sweetness, acidity and bitterness; soft, relaxed and therefore fruity taste-aromas; augmentative a merit because a wine has wide nose and mouth when it has an optimal equilibrium.

Wine blendings: mixture of diverse wines.

WINE-FRUIT: *neologism, wine with a superior index of technical and analytical quality, therefore with a taste of absolute pleasantness. Wine-fruit is the wine emblematically representative of the pulpy, mature and uncontaminated grape just picked up and therefore universally pleasant. It is in practice the ideal wine, didactic and propaedeutical, that all the people who say to be abstemiouses and not to know how to appreciate a wine should taste. This because the pulpy, soft and intact fruitiness – which is the pleasantness of the taste of a wine-fruit – can be nothing but immediately and spontaneously appreciated by the entire universe of human* *beings. Just in the same way in which the grape has always been appreciated.*

Wrung: vinous liquid resulting from the wringing of marcs; very rich in tannins it is often added to red wines poor in colour and extractive substances to strengthen their hue and structure.

Y

Year: year of production

Other LM Publication

Available in the best libraries or by mail care of LM

ANNUARIO DEI
MIGLIORI VINI ITALIANI
The best wines of Italy described and evaluated point by point
750 pages, 379 Luca Maroni's organoleptical schedules,
379 viticultural and oenological schedules, 379 reproduced labels
Profiles and addresses of productive firms.
Bookbinding in precious cloth with gold impressions
Size cm 15 x cm 23,5

GUIDE TO
ITALIAN WINES
The most important Italian wine firms analysed wine by wine.
2016 pages, 12196 tasted wines,
1895 wine estates, 140 pages of classifications,
List of Wine-fruit, 206.147 total items of information.
Bookbinding in plasticised glossy paper, two-coloured print
Pocket size cm 11,5 x cm 20

THE TASTER OF WINE
Magazine to know and appreciate wine and tasting
48 pages, more than 300 Italian and foreign tasted wines per number, interviews, updatings on tasting technique, dialogue with readers, thoughts on wine.
Size cm 21 x cm 28,5
QUARTERLY AND BY SUBSCRIPTION

TASTING
WINE
Handbook of Theory and Practice
The method to evaluate the pleasantness-fruitiness of any wine.
Includes a user manual and tasting notebook with 140 tables for personal tasting notes.
Plasticised paperback printed in two color.
Pocket size cm 10 x cm 14